The Arctic 1927

A. Y. Jackson
The Arctic 1927

Introduction by Naomi Jackson Groves

PENUMBRA PRESS, 1982

Contents

Introduction by Naomi Jackson Groves
From The Far North, by Dr. F.G. Banting
The First Diary, 1927A
The Plates
The Second Diary, 1927B
List of Drawings

Copyright © PENUMBRA PRESS, 1982.

Published by PENUMBRA PRESS, P.O. Box 340, Moonbeam, Ontario, Canada POL 1VO with financial assistance from The Canada Council and The Ontario Arts Council. The typeface is Trump Medieval and the stock is Zephyr Antique Laid. Printed at The Porcupine's Quill, Inc.

ISBN 0 920806 37 6

Dedicated to all who love the North and in honour of
the A.Y. Jackson Centennial, 1882-1982

The year 1982 is special for A.Y. Jackson enthusiasts for it is the centenary of his birth. With this publication of drawings and journals from 55 years ago, Penumbra Press is proud to celebrate a small part of his northern output.

THE ARCTIC 1927 was prepared for the press by Naomi Jackson Groves, who also wrote the introduction. We are indebted to many galleries and collectors and institutions which graciously permitted some of their drawings by A.Y. Jackson to be reproduced for this book – Alberta Art Foundation, Edmonton; the McMichael Canadian Collection, Kleinburg; National Gallery of Canada, Ottawa; Norman MacKenzie Art Gallery, Regina; Firestone Art Collection, Ottawa; Winnipeg Art Gallery; and various private collectors, especially Miss Else Bjarne of Denmark. We would also like to thank Rous and Mann, Limited for permission to reprint Dr. F.G. Banting's introduction from *The Far North* (1928).

Introduction

Alexander Young Jackson, who would have been one hundred years old on October 3, 1982, visited the northeastern Arctic three times: by boat in 1927 and 1930, when he was in his forties, and by air in 1965, when he was nearly eighty-three.

Jackson was the first professional Canadian artist to work in that area and, considering the difficult working conditions, produced a considerable body of work. In 1927, our present concern, he brought back dozens of drawings both in pencil (black graphite and the occasional conté crayon) and some twenty in pen and ink; about forty sketches in oil paint on wood panels approximately 8 ½ x 10 ½ inches in size (sometimes made on the boat from the quick drawings when there was no chance to stay long enough in one spot or when the weather was too wet and foggy outdoors). And finally he produced the six or more canvases painted later in Toronto.

In addition, Jackson wrote daily entries as a sort of 'journal' on each of the journeys by boat. On the 1927 trip he actually kept two diaries simultaneously. One (referred to technically as '1927 A') was for himself and consists of seven foolscap pages 10 x 6 inches, written in pencil on one side of the paper, in a very casual style with minimal sentence structure, few capitals, no punctuation except a sort of comma-period-dash which marks the end of a phrase or thought. This style is partially retained here for '1927 A,' which gives more daily information about numbers of drawings and sketches, bits of conversation to be remembered, etc.

The second diary ('1927 B') seems to have been written mainly for Jackson's Toronto friends, F.B. (Fred) Housser and his wife Bess, who later became the second Mrs. Lawren Harris. This version, likewise in pencil with occasional marginal remarks added in ink, is on 25 pages measuring 7 ½ x 5 inches, numbered 1-26 (his page 24, covering parts of August 29 and 30, is missing). Sentence structure is somewhat less casual than in the 'A' version, and has been furnished here with a few capitals, periods and commas.

There is surprisingly little repetition in the two 1927 manuscripts. 'B' starts only on July 24, eight days after the *Beothic* had sailed from Sydney, Nova Scotia, and by chance omits one day (August 14) in addition to the missing page 24; however, 'B' gives more description of landscape, ice conditions, etc. Each contains entrancing details not included in the other, and maintains its own pace, so rather than to be chopped up and patched together, each will be given here in full.

The pencil drawings for the 1927 trip come in three main sizes and types of paper – one relatively large, two smaller. Jackson must have taken along a single loose-leaf holder with two rings, into which he fitted some drawing sheets left over from 1926 and spring 1927, measuring 8 ⅜ x 10 ⅞ inches, with three machine-made holes on the long side, the centre one of which remained intact when he jerked the drawing out of the covers. More numerous are pages of firm, cream-coloured paper which had been hand-cut or torn from a larger sheet into halves sometimes uneven, with heights varying between 7 ½ and 8 ⅜ inches, and width approximately 11 ¼. Some pages have been pushed forcibly onto the two loose-leaf rings, others without holes were merely laid into the sketchbook then removed; all these have one rough long side, usually the top of the drawing. It can be noted that none is as large as the 1930 drawings, which present records show to have all been 9 x 12 inches. In the 'larger' 1927 drawings, the rich, dark effects of the 5B graphite pencil can be appreciated in full-size reproduction in the book, *A.Y.'s Canada*, Clarke, Irwin 1968. The present volume shows, almost full-size, the two smaller 1927 sizes, in sequence as close as possible to the order in which they were done (both sizes mingled): the one approximately 5 ½ x 9 inches on semi-translucent smooth paper with a serrated long edge where the drawing has been separated from its sketchbook, and two rounded corners opposite. The smallest size is 5 x 8 inches, on firm paper showing no holes or serration, so likely from a pad glued across one small end.

Some of the 1927 drawings are inscribed with exact location and date. The fact that the artist many years later added '1930' in ink to some of his 1927 drawings need not be too confusing. The *Beothic* left Sydney 15 days later in 1930 than in 1927, so the actual dates at various ports of call tended to be very different, as well of course as the different sizes of paper used on the two journeys.

On board the *Beothic* during the 1927 voyage, Jackson made a number of pen-and-ink drawings which were included in the exhibition he held at the Art Gallery of Toronto that September. They were published the following year by Rous and Mann, Toronto, in the fine little vivid-green-covered book, *The Far North*. One thousand copies were announced but Jackson is recorded as saying that only five hundred were actu-

Bylot Island

ally printed. There are seventeen plates, with descriptive text for each, plus two vignettes, one for the title page and one below the Introduction written by Jackson's travelling companion, Dr. Frederick Banting. The latter's text is well suited to the present volume, as is the pen-and-ink map which Jackson included to show their route.

Ottawa, March 1982   *Naomi Jackson Groves*

From The Far North*

The *Beothic* left Sydney on the 16th of July, 1927, bound for Godhavn, Greenland, afterward calling at the various posts established by the Royal Canadian Mounted Police, relieving men who had been on duty two years, and leaving provisions and coal for a year. The Pond Inlet settlement was to be the first objective but ice conditions made it impossible to get in until over two weeks later on the return journey. We called at the North Devon Island post first, then after a short stay at Etah in Greenland, the steamer went on to the Bache Peninsula where the most northerly station in the world is maintained. Turning south to Lancaster Sound we went westward along the historic channel until the ice pack off Cornwallis Island stopped us.

After calling at Somerset Island and Arctic Bay on Baffin Island, Pond Inlet was found to be free of ice. Pangnirtung was the next post visited, then Lake Harbour, Wakeham Bay and Port Burwell, all on Hudson Strait.

The *Beothic*, twenty-seven hundred tons, was American-built, length reduced at bow and stern, and heavily plated in England for ice breaking. Her commander, Capt. Falke, was born within the Arctic circle in Norway, and has spent years navigating in the ice. Mr. G.P. Mackenzie who was in charge of the expedition has lived thirty years in the Yukon, and the 'mounties' were all men familiar with the far north.

* Reprinted from *The Far North, A Book of Drawings* by A.Y. Jackson, Toronto, Rous and Mann, Limited [1928].

Through the courtesy of the Minister of the Interior, A.Y. Jackson, artist of Toronto, a member of the Group of Seven, was invited to go.

It is a privilege to write a foreword to this book of drawings, since it was my good fortune to accompany the expedition; and seeing the country, I can vouch for the artist's sincerity.

Sketching was done under considerable difficulty; cold and wind would have chilled the enthusiasm of a less ardent worker. Jackson cherishes an illusion that the finest colour is generally to be found on the most exposed spots. A restless desire to find what lies beyond the distant hills makes it hard to keep up with him. The barren wastes proved to be rich in form and colour, strange rhythms and unexpected vistas. During our all too brief and exciting scrambles ashore, he would be chuckling and laughing all day – a mood I found contagious.

On the ship he would watch the changing landscape, following the wind-blown clouds, drinking in the beauty of colour of the coast formations, and studying the subtle effects of light on the moving ice.

To travel up the North Pole route to Kane Basin, then along the old North-West passage route of Lancaster Sound, and then into Hudson Strait all in one short summer, is perhaps a superficial way of seeing the Arctic, but I feel that much of the spirit of the country is expressed in these drawings.

F.G. Banting

The First Diary, 1927 A

July 16th 1927

Beothic sailed shortly after noon. We were photographed in the drizzling rain for the Toronto Star. The seven RCMPs who are going up to relieve the various posts, then the other members of the expedition, G.P. Mackenzie, Dr. Banting, Dr. Stringer, Dr. Malte, the botanist, and self. As we pulled out, Banting tore off his collar and threw it overboard, calling out: 'No more white collars!' The rotund and jovial Malte followed with his, and then Stringer. It made the departure quite dramatic. The Mayor of North Sydney and other notables were on the dock to bid us farewell.

We ran into drizzle, passed Cape North in the late evening; quiet sea yellow grey, whales to the westward. Nearly all northern Canadians – Stringer born on Herschell Id. All the Mounties go up again to various posts. Captain Falke has almost lived on ice, from Wrangell Id., Hudson Bay, Kane Basin and all the other ice resorts. The police are good types, one wonders what takes such young chaps away to places where all the usual things young fellows like are denied them. There is not even fame. Got a lot of toy balloons, colored crayons, candy and such things for the Esquimaux.

Sunday July 17th

Sea calm, sun seeping through misty sky. Mackenzie speaking about the various commissions, told of a man at the mouth of the Mackenzie sending word to Ottawa to send a suit of clothes to his son up in Greenland. We have two pigs aboard, bound for one of the ports in Baffin Land. The natives in Greenland live under a paternal form of government. All trade is a government monopoly; no private traders are allowed, all profits are returned to the natives, prices of furs are kept low, as the Danish government realize what a calamity it would be to exterminate game. Fishing on the other hand is encouraged.

Later. Sea like glass all day. Sunny, sitting on the deck reading, following Newfoundland coast about twenty miles off. Everything fine. Moonrise over Newfoundland, pale aurora opposite. One of the police who was at North Devon two years tells me the aurora is seldom visible there – a pale shimmering directly overhead or to the southward.

Monday July 18th	Foggy. Going through Belle Isle. First ice berg, shrouded in fog, glint of light on the prow. A whole succession of bergs, we were kept busy trying to make drawings of them. Remarkable diversity of forms. Labrador coast visible about 2.00; Ship starting to roll. The farm yard on the after deck climbed up on the hatches, as the deck was awash. A couple of roosters, about twenty hens and two pigs.
Tuesday	Cold foggy [illegible]. Mal de mer. ship rolling, not much zest.
Wednesday	Still under the weather. Nothing to see. Banting up reading all night.
Thursday	Almost better, but a heavy sea came up and the *Beothic* rolls.
Friday	Quieter. more ducks and gulls. Sighted Greenland about 2.30, big hills, grey and snow capped.
Saturday July 23rd	Slid into Godhavn out of the fog. cold but sunny. got up about six, made a couple of drawings. The governor, wireless operator and others came aboard. Esquimo kayaks. wireless man in straw hat, said it was the first chance to wear it. Went ashore, made two sketches. Had lunch on rocks. Fête day for the village. Left at 5 PM, kept along the Disco coast, high and severe, passed ice bergs, no night, flowers small but different, except Pyrola.
Sunday July 24th	Grey day, windless. Greenland coast faint in distance. few small bergs. clouds mostly cirrus and distant stratus. Wilcox tells me they have ravens in Ellesmere Island all the year. Noranda [shares] $22.40. A message from a girl to one of the Mounties got on the radio: 'Have been sick. spent Christmas in bed. Missed you very much.'
Monday July 25th	Pushing through Melville ice pack all day. Sunny after breakfast, but low-lying fog bank came up from south. Pushing towards Pond Inlet, ice fairly open. Made two sketches and a drawing.
Tuesday	Pack opened up and weather cleared. Bylot Id. high mts and Baffin Id. came in

sight. Bright but cool. fog bank obscured channel to Pond Inlet. Fog lifted and we started up the channel. shores sombre. rocky ridges running to sharp peaks. red rock in places. Channel blocked with a solid line of ice. waited till midnight for word from post, and left for North Devon. Inspector Wilcox to stay until we return from Lancaster Sound.

Wednesday
July 27th

Mild weather, half sunlight. followed the Bylot coast. hundreds of mountains, deeply covered with snow. shoreline wide in places. only one glacier out of many reached water. Foggy after lunch. reached Dundas, North Devon in evening. There policemen all well, went ashore. foggy and drizzly, lots of flowers, saxifrage, heather, blueberry, poppies, etc. Police have about fifty dogs. Dr. Malte stayed on shore.

Thursday
July 28th

Went ashore. made a sketch in drizzle. left after lunch, followed coast of North Devon. very exciting. made drawings all the afternoon.

Friday
July 29th

Went in to Craig Harbour, Ellesmere. Full of ice, fog cutting off all the tops of hills. Mounties went ashore over ice. Tried to sketch off steamer, which moved all over the place. Left for Etah about 2 P.M. (*verso* of page: Dr. Svendsden of the Fram died on the north side of entrance to Hayes Fiord.) weather quiet. sea smooth. full of ice. many seals lying on the ice. lots of ducks. Coburg Island smothered in clouds. interesting. as we swung round to the east coast of Ellesmere, the country gets severer. glaciers in every valley. most of them reaching the sea. deep snow over everything. there seems to be no vegetation. Further on we got into fields of icebergs, some very large ones. weather cold, foggy. very little sunlight so far.

Saturday
July 30th

Decks covered with snow this morning. foggy and rainy all day. walrus on the ice floes. Nosed into Etah out of a thick fog. blew whistle. four tents at Etah. took two Eskimo families on board, gave all the others a feed, and sweaters. millions of birds.

Sunday
July 31st

Left at 6:30 for Rice Straits. drizzle and fog. great country if we could see it. Made drawing of Fram Harbour, where we expected to land Sgt. Joy. no one there. passed

Pim and Cocked Hat Island. sea clear of ice in Kane Basin. found all well. went ashore. Mackinson and Anstead took over post with Garnett. Mountains all covered with fog.

|Monday August 1st| Caught in ice pack. made only a half mile in nine hours. got in lee of island, while ice drifted past. got out at 2 PM and put on all steam for Rice Straits. rain and fog.

|Tuesday August 2nd| Fog and snow. making for Craig Harbour. cleared up after lunch. harbour about free of ice. went ashore. climbed hill to west, over to Fram Fiord. made sketch at 11.30. returned over big field of boulders, covered with [illegible] and lichens. stunted poppies and magenta saxifrage. the latter very rich in color. got back to post Sgt. Joy made us coffee. left about 1 AM. ice forming on the bay.

|Wednesday August 3rd| On the way to Dundas. following along the S. Devon coast. Weather fine. sun so bright we got out our smoked glasses. arrived at Dundas about 7 PM. went ashore. Esquimos moving household effects on board. light bright but colorless. went in for a bathe. made a sketch. returned to Post. RCMP Wilson made supper for us.

|Thursday August 4th| Along Lancaster Sound. grey. drizzling. following west coast of N. Devon desolate. red grey sandstone. terraced. flat on top. some places like vast coloseum, half circles. going through to Melville if possible. Inspector Wilcox speaks of getting money at Pond Inlet. Great hilarity when Ketchum said he was told the white whale comes in to shore to scratch himself, but this was verified by Sgt White. they come into the sandy bays and wallow around until the sand scrapes all the slime and barnacles off them. it takes a week or two. but they come in yellow and dirty and are quite white when they get through. Later: Fog and heavy seas. compasses get useless here. and we turned into Beechey to wait. bay full of ice. we anchored outside of it. The small relief ship left for Franklin is still on the beach. a great pile of sheer rock about a thousand feet high rises from the water. to the eastward it descends in a series of shale hills, leaving a miserable little beach at the foot, where Franklin and his men made their winter quarters. (*verso* of page: Beechey Id. 639 feet high. Somerset is Silurian, except Archaean on west coast. The *Arctic* at the end of Aug and beginning of Sept 1908 passed through Barrow

quarters. Thu Aug. 5th Still storm bound. a big ice field from the south has come across & is crowding us in. we had to up anchor this morning and again this afternoon, to get out of its way. Capt Fakke telling us about the wreck of the Lady Kindersley, caught in the ice north of Alaska. they tried to blow it up with gasoline. instead of intending for explosives. poured gasoline on boats in it and set it on fire. lifted the anchors up as desired thrown it. After 4½ days they were rescued by the Boxer. left the L.K. in the ice and walked over the ice to the Boxer.

Fri Aug 6th Bright and sunny. but bay full of ice. we broke thru't a open space and got ashore in the motor boat. made two drawings of the cliffs at Beechey. shore covered with debris. burnt stoves old rusty tins. canvas etc. ruined winter quarters of Franklin & later Belcher not showing effects of time or weather. James who was later murdered. tore everything down. monument taken up by Kane left at Disco. put up by McClintock. repaired 1906 by Bernier. Memorial attached also to Bellot. water barrels still good. could be used. partly ground frozen. Later ice kept coming in all afternoon. dragging our anchors. we have to push them if every hour or so. no sign of open water. fog obscuring everything. Sgt Joy sketching about the musky islands. found lots of game. caribou fat in the autumn. but so thin in the spring he did not know how they could live. they could walk right up to them. lots of musk ox. the dogs can smell them three or four miles away. he could scent them a mile or a half. lots of lemmings. and foxes & wolves. mostly white. Ringes Island very barren. N. ends Ellesmere has some vegetation inland a little ways. Big concert.

Sunday Aug. 7th Foggy. still at Beechey Island. bay full of ice. fog cleared this later and we started out. lost in fog for awhile. in the afternoon fog lifted and we could see Cornwallis. sea like a mirror. ice field on Cornwallis for ten miles out. and north and south as far as we could see. we turned south following the pack. then east. fields of ice drifting in water. saw two walruses.

Monday Aug 8th Hung around all night. in the fog. it lifted towards noon and we found ourselves off Lowther Island. where James Ross wintered in 1848-49. we pushed on to Port Leopold. where there is a recently formed H.B. post. which is highly going to close up. we are awaiting instructions about taking them off. two white men Jordan and Nichol. and a lot of Labrador natives. a rotten unpicturesque outfit. living in wedgetents and stove cloths. the landscape & winter utter desolation. every virtue the everlasting fog hanging over it. Stumic took turns out about fish by trout. no moss or even lichen to relieve it. a very few stunted flowers. poppies. mustard (draba) saxifrage etc. forms a meagre and poor vegetation. The country from a distance looked a little like Southern Alberta. the cliffs supporting dry grass. Sgt Joy sketching & discovered in the Arctic and finding a large sprinkling lying across a shale ravine about two or three hundred feet above sea level on a small island off the west coast of Ellesmere. also of the quantities of musk ox excretions that seem to have hardened into stone. of the flesh eating walruses. that have the seal and seldom come above water. their habitat is off the south east of Ellesmere. Musk ox increasing. Sunflower of Pearys took heavy toll of them. but they will probably push thru that yet.

Tue Aug 9th Have gone in for archeology. this morning it was foggy so we went ashore I wore ingles and did some excavating. Sgt Joy says they are not very ancient. about 150 yrs. found a few bone implements. afternoon went ashore again & made drawings of two inglos. Sgt Joy

Strait, without difficulty and in a few days reached McClure Strait to find it quite clear of ice. They could probably have made the N.W. passage.

Prince Patrick Id. Lieut.[?] Micham[?]. 1853. McClintock Expedition explored found decayed wood. 90 feet above ice. which appeared to have grown there. Further inland he found parts of trees, bark in perfect condition. one tree was 2 feet 10 in diameter. On Banks Id. quantities of wood were found by McClure. 500 ft above sea level, in good enough condition to be cut up and used for fuel. One trunk sticking out of a ravine measured 42 in in circumference.

Port Leopold. cliffs. yellowish tinted limestone. First visited by Sir James Ross 20 Aug to 30th Sept 1832 again in Sept 1848. Eskimo had all been abandoned prior to 1832. (Wilcox) Have you any fish?)

Friday August 5th	Still storm bound. a big ice field from the south has come across and is crowding us in. We had to up anchor this morning and again in the afternoon, to get out of its way. Capt Falke telling us about the wreck of the *Lady Kindersley*, caught in the ice north of Alaska. They tried to blow it up with gasoline, emptied out cartridges for explosives, poured gasoline in pools on it and set it on fire. Lifted the anchors up and dropped them on it. After 24 days they were rescued by the *Boxer*, left the L.K. in the ice and walked over the ice to the *Boxer*.
Saturday August 6th	Bright and sunny, but bay full of ice. We broke through to an open space and got ashore in the motor boat. Made two drawings of the cliffs and Marie. Shore covered with debris, barrel staves old rusty tins, canvas etc. ruined winter quarters of Franklin and later Belcher not showing effects of time or weather. Janes, who was later murdered, tore everything down. Monument taken up by Kane left at Disco, and put up by McClintock, repaired 1906 by Bernier. Monument attached also to Bellot. Water barrels still good, could be used, partly gnawed by bears. Later: ice kept coming in all afternoon, dragging our anchors. We have to push through it every hour or so. No sign of open water, fog obscuring everything. Sgt Joy speaking about the western islands, found lots of game – caribou, fat in the autumn, but so thin in the spring he did not see how they would live. They could walk right up to them. Lots of muskox, the dogs can smell them three or four

miles away; he could scent them a mile and a half. Lots of lemmings, and foxes and wolves, mostly white. Ringes Island very barren. N. Cornwallis has some vegetation inland a little way. Dog concert.

Sunday
August 7th

Foggy, still at Beechey Island, bay full of ice. It cleared up later and we started out, lost in fog for a while. In the afternoon, fog lifted and we could see Cornwallis, sea like a mirror. Ice piled on Cornwallis for ten miles out, and north and south as far as we could see. We turned south, following the pack, then east. Film of ice forming on water. Saw two walrus.

Monday
August 8th

Hung around all night in the fog. It lifted towards noon and we found ourselves off Leopold Island, where James Ross wintered in 1848-49. We pushed on to Port Leopold, where there is a recently formed H.B. post, which is probably going to close up. We are awaiting instructions about taking them off – two white men, Jardine and Nichol, and a lot of Labrador natives, a rather unpicturesque outfit, living in wedge tents and store clothes. The landscape is uninteresting desolation, even without the everlasting fog hanging over it. Silurian rock broken into sharp flakes by frost, no moss or even lichen to relieve it. A very few stunted flowers, poppies, mustard (darba [?]) saxifrage etc formed a meagre and rare vegetation. The country from a distance looked a little like Southern Alberta, the shale suggesting dry grass. Sgt Joy, speaking of driftwood in the Arctic, mentioned finding a large spruce log, lying across a small ravine about two or three hundred feet above sea level on a small island off the west coast of Ellesmere, also of the quantities of musk ox excretions that seem to have hardened into stone. of the flesh eating walrus that hunt the seal and seldom come above water. their habitat is off the south end of Ellesmere. Musk ox increasing. Sverdrup and Peary took heavy toll of them but they will probably push through ... to band again soon

Tuesday
August 9th

Have gone in for archeology. this morning it was foggy so we went ashore to some ingloos [sic!] and did some excavating. Sgt Joy says they are not very ancient, about 150 years. Found a few bone implements. After lunch went ashore again and made drawings of the ingloos. (verso of page: Birds. Aukpak black back, head and tip of tail, creamy white body, grey white under wings. scud along the water clumsily using their wings, probably dwarf penguins. Little Auk, similiar to above much smaller. Sea Pigeon. black, white spots on wings, red feet. Small bluish white gull, like tern. Dundas. Large black bird, gull shaped, legs hang out behind like heron. Ravens at Craig Harbour. Small bird similar to snow bunting. Gulls, light fawn, uneven, with lighter spots on wings. Bird blackish, like large swallow or small tern.) Had seal for supper. Windy, cold. Leopold Island visible, nesting place for sea pigeon and aukpak.

Wednesday August 10th

We are not going to Melville, but east again to Arctic Bay and Pond Inlet. Rain wind and fog. Made pen drawings of ingloo. H.B. people coming on board, closing post.

Thursday August 11th

Left for Arctic Bay. big sea running but we are running into it and the *Beothic* stands a head sea very well. turned into Admiralty Inlet. Land between Leopold and Admiralty plateau. few small dead glaciers, terraced. Sgt. Joy says there is scarcely a blade of grass the whole way across. Shores of Admiralty Inlet on east very fine, succession of Gothic churches and strongholds, rosy in color. arrived Arctic Harbour about 2 AM, sunset and twilight.

Friday August 12th

Went ashore at 3 AM with Banting and Malte. Made sketch, walked along beach. traces of summer camps, flat stones for floors, and rings of rocks for tents. Met Eskimo at H.B. factors. Had to shake hands all round. Ladies tattooed. Returned to steamer. Eskimos came out on ice which had closed in, wonderful exhibition of ice jumping. Chauve Souris costumes. Fifteen natives died of starvation down Admiralty Inlet, Shinik Islands, children probably eaten – no traces of them. remarkable cliff at entrance to Arctic Bay.

Saturday August 13th

Tried to get to Pond Inlet by Navy Board Channel. still frozen over. have to go round Bylot. sunny, calm. Sgt. Joy talking about Canada's Arctic expeditions, said they have not had results of any importance, expensive and often dishonest, rotten supplies sent to police posts, broke five axe handles getting blubber, rotten wood supplied for komatiks. sugar full of sand and dirt, punk binoculars. wanted to explore Lake Hazen, and early settlements. and go round north shore of Ellesmere. Lewis Bros the only honest tools supplied to posts. Pups fed every three days. Made drawings of Eskimos.

Sunday
August 14th

Went ashore. Bright sunlight all day. miles of rolling pasture land, ponds and streams. wandered round all day, made two sketches, went to see old igloos [sic!], then to Police Barracks. Corp Pettie made supper for me. sketched Eskimo house. slept at barracks. Joy talks of husky habits

Monday
August 15th

Foggy, later rainy. picked plants. had fresh salmon. boat returned from Albert Harbour. went on board. Murray came in to cabin and talked about police. Berg nearly bumped into steamer. One of the boys told of the H.B. selling an Eskimo a violin and a barrel of resin for the strings.

Tuesday
August 16th

Steamer fooled round all morning and until 3 PM on account of ice. went ashore, made sketch. last of supplies hurried over. bay full of motor boats. Left about nine. Wilcox, Margetts and Cox stayed at post.

Wednesday
August 17th

On way home. heading south off Baffin Land coast. from Pond Inlet for sixty miles forms rounded. Later: sharp peaks, high country, sunny and clear. on way to Clyde. Sketched huskies. Joy says, like humans, dogs of one family will make a fine team, but if they don't agree, the fights are far more bitter than among a mixed team. (*verso* of page: Pond Inlet – tertiary. Disko Island – Archaean overlaid with tertiary. Dunn to Dr Banting: 'Hey, Doc, are you the guy that has the Edgeworth?'
   The Husky dog has brought up a most complex legal problem when food is scarce he claims the ownership of his own excrement, but being at a decided disadvantage, his comrades get it first.
   Dr Livingstone says that he believes that white foxes have as many as 17 pups.
   South Baffin Land. Archaean Rock (granites gneisses, and other crystallines). ¾ of Baffin Archaean.) Later: grand evening, mirage of icebergs. Saw two polar bears. Light on southern half of sky.

Thursday
August 18th

Getting in to Clyde. full of ice. passed a piece of ice with tons of earth and boulders piled on it. Clyde not exciting. went ashore, climbed hill with Banting, made sketch. whistle blew in the middle of it, had to hurry back to beach. Joy and White both find raw frozen meat very appetizing – frozen seal blubber and caribou meat. Keeps the teeth very clean. Clyde once a great caribou country, but none left. Eskimo let their dogs run loose in summer and the young fawns are killed off.

Friday
August 19th

Cold and foggy, everyone asleep. On way to Pangnirtung out of sight of land. Passed close to a very large berg, about 9 PM Irresponsibility of Eskimo. Sgt White told of a chap paying an Eskimo fifty dollars to stock up his meat supply as he had only two seals. he came back two months later and found the Eskimo had used up the two seals.

Saturday

Cold. No one on deck, only distant coast visible.

Sunday
August 21st

Passed Saxe Coburg Id. running along north shore of Cumberland Sound. fine undulating country, almost clear of snow. arrived at Pangnirtung after supper. Jenkins came out in kayak; Weeks and Haycock still away. went shore, made sketch. Clouds over hills up the bay.

Monday
August 22nd

Went ashore, waded over tops of my Dack boots. foggy, drizzle most of the day. Made drawings of Eskimo houses. Went back for about three miles with Banting. Country covered with boulders and deep moss. flowers going to seed, less variety than further north, found bear berries. went to Police Post for supper of aukpak eggs and baked potatoes. Cook Timberley. played deck tennis, went on board. had to listen to Mr Dunn. He told us about the difficulties of issuing marriage licences to Eskimos. one woman tried to cash hers at the H.B. post as a wolf bounty. Movie show, most of Pangnirtung came on board. great enthusiasm when the Pangnirtung people were shown, also for an imitation of Felix the Cat.

Tuesday

Left at daybreak, fog and rain all day. No land visible. On way to Lake Harbour.

Wednesday

Very foggy in night. on way to Hudson Straits.

Thursday

Fair, good run. passed Big Island, picked up pilot. coast all broken up with islands.

                    H.B. post and church. Atkinson away on leave. went ashore, rich vegetation – buttercups, dandelions, arnica, blue berries, bear berries about ripe. made sketch. drizzle in air.

Friday August 26th   Off for the day with Banting. rain in morning, grey all day. great variety to country, lakes everywhere. rocks full of mica. former caribou country, but only old bones and horns left. Lots of lemming holes but have not seen any yet. New Police barracks going up rapidly. (*verso* of page: koolatak. At Port Burwell, wood is used for fuel. driftwood from Hudson Bay is found along Ungava Bay, and wood is also procured about 30 or 40 miles inland.)

Saturday August 27th   Went ashore. Sunshine for an hour. went west, lots of lakes. climbed ridge overlooking valley. big chain of lakes running towards sea. very windy, cold and grey. made 3 sketches. flowers – white saxifrage, arctic cotton, fire weed, pyrola. Saw a large rabbit, white, dabs of black. Made fire to call attention of *Beothic*.

Sunday August 28th   Sunny, went ashore. behind new post. did a lot of wandering without finding a composition. Left at 3 PM for Wakeham Bay. Sgt White and Paul Dursh stayed at post. Sea quiet, faint aurora.

Monday August 29th   Woke up in Wakeham Bay. Larch and Stanley in port. Went ashore, carried from boat by Lawrence. feeling sad about the loss of their Moth plane. Met Carr Harris, gang of 30 carpenters obeying union rules, making slow progress with buildings. other post at Nottingham Island, and third post at Burwell, but nothing done. Left about 10 AM grey day, quiet sea, very dark. going half speed towards Cape Chidley.

Tuesday August 30th   Heavy fog, had difficulty finding Port Burwell. we passed schooner with a tow, and got into Burwell about 3 PM interesting rock. H.B. Post, Air Station, old Moravian Mission ... country very broken up, full of lakes. big granite boulders lying everywhere. good cod fishing. cold and bleak. scantier vegetation than Lake Harbour, Pangnirtung or Pond Inlet. Nichols and Montague, RCMP staying on another year. Cogshill, two other airmen and D. Kelly also staying. fine aurora, big spirals.

Wednesday August 31st	Went ashore with Banting, made sketch. color very interesting – ice on pools in rocks. big sea pounding on the coast. had to return to steamer at eleven, left after lunch – got a tossing before getting between Button Islands and Cape Chidley. coast very bold, from Chidley south. bright sunlight. Aurora at night, mild.
Thursday September 1st	Labrador in extreme distance this AM, out of sight of land since. sea quiet, weather mild. made 2 sketches. ate the pig, our shipmate.
Friday September 2nd	Bright sunlight all day. sea quiet, lights of Labrador coast visible in evening. Joy thinks Steffanson most remarkable Arctic traveller, in spite of his verbosity. not a very high opinion of MacMillan, he is not liked generally in north. Rasmussen very much respected. admires Anderson at Ottawa.
Saturday September 3rd	Foggy all day. Went through Belle Isle without seeing any land. packing up. night, steamer whistling every few minutes.

The Plates

Plate 1　*The Beothic at Sydney, Nova Scotia*

Plate 2 *The Beothic, Sydney*, N.S.

Plate 3 *The Beothic at Sydney,* N.S.

Plate 4 *The Stern of the Beothic*

Plate 5
First Icebergs, Belle Isle

Plate 6 *Icebergs and Mirage*

Plate 7
Four Icebergs

Plate 8 *Icebergs on Skyline near Godhavn, Greenland*

Plate 9 *Icebergs at Godhavn*

Plate 10   *Godhavn, Eskimo House*

Plate 11 *Dark House in Godhavn*

Plate 12 *Pushing Through Melville Pack Ice*

Plate 13 *Towards Pond Inlet, Ice and Fog*

Plate 14　*Mirage*

Plate 15 *Bylot near Pond Inlet*

Plate 16 *Baffin North of Pond*

Plate 17   *Above Pond Inlet, Baffin*

Plate 18 *Dundas Harbor, July 27th*

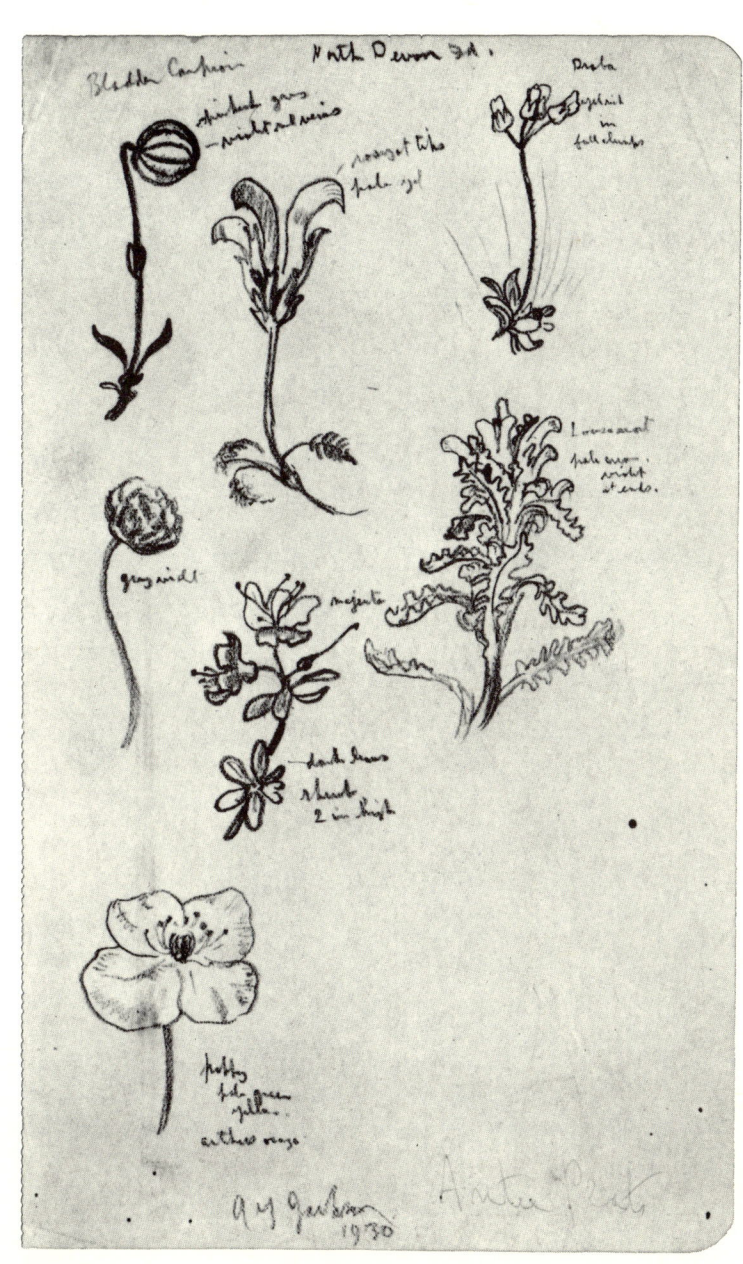

Plate 19
Arctic Plants, North Devon Island

Plate 20 *Coburg Island*

Plate 21   *North Devon Island*

Plate 22 *Etah, Greenland*

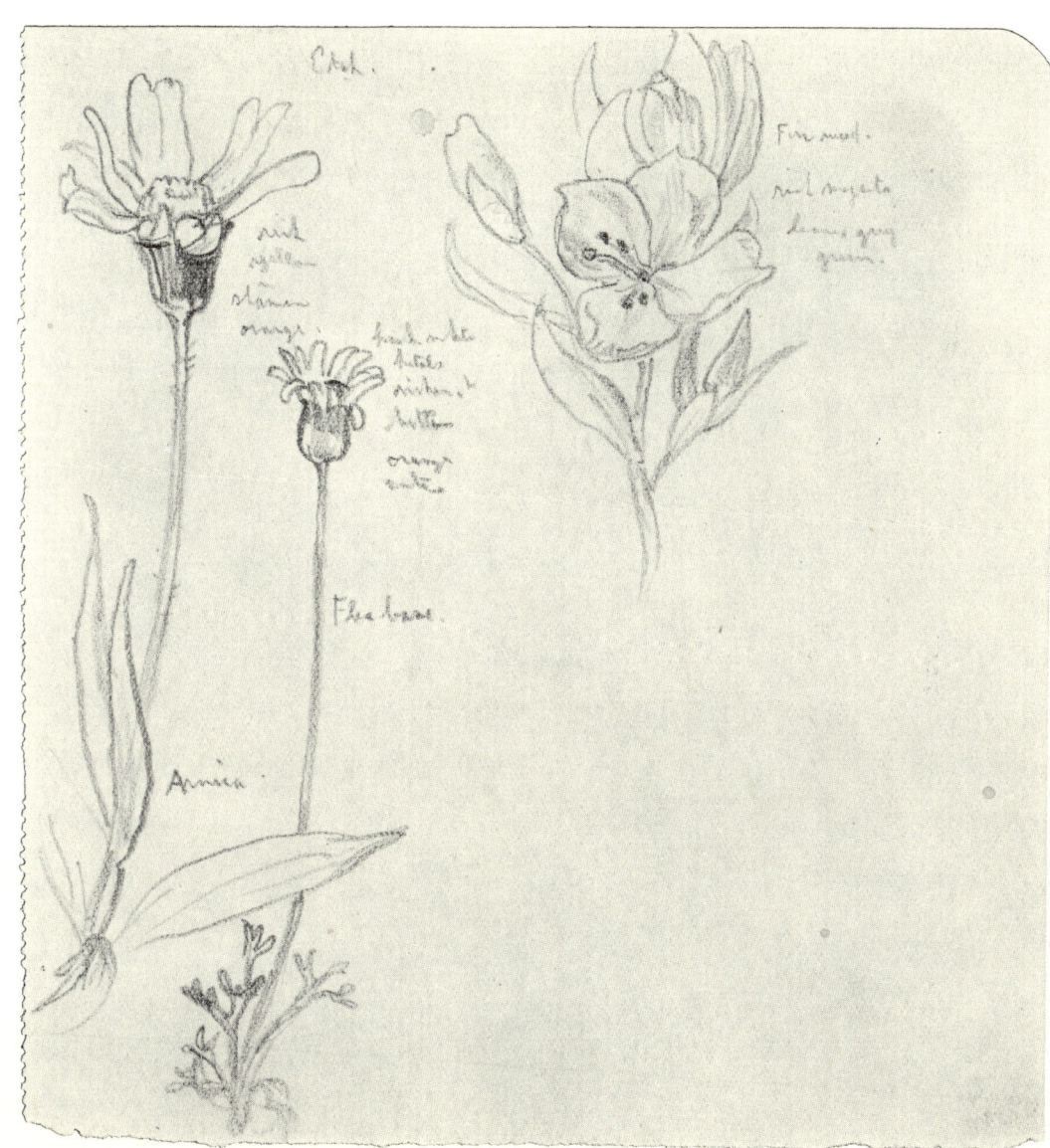

Plate 23 *Flower Studies, Etah, Greenland*

Plate 24 *Etah, Greenland, summer camp*

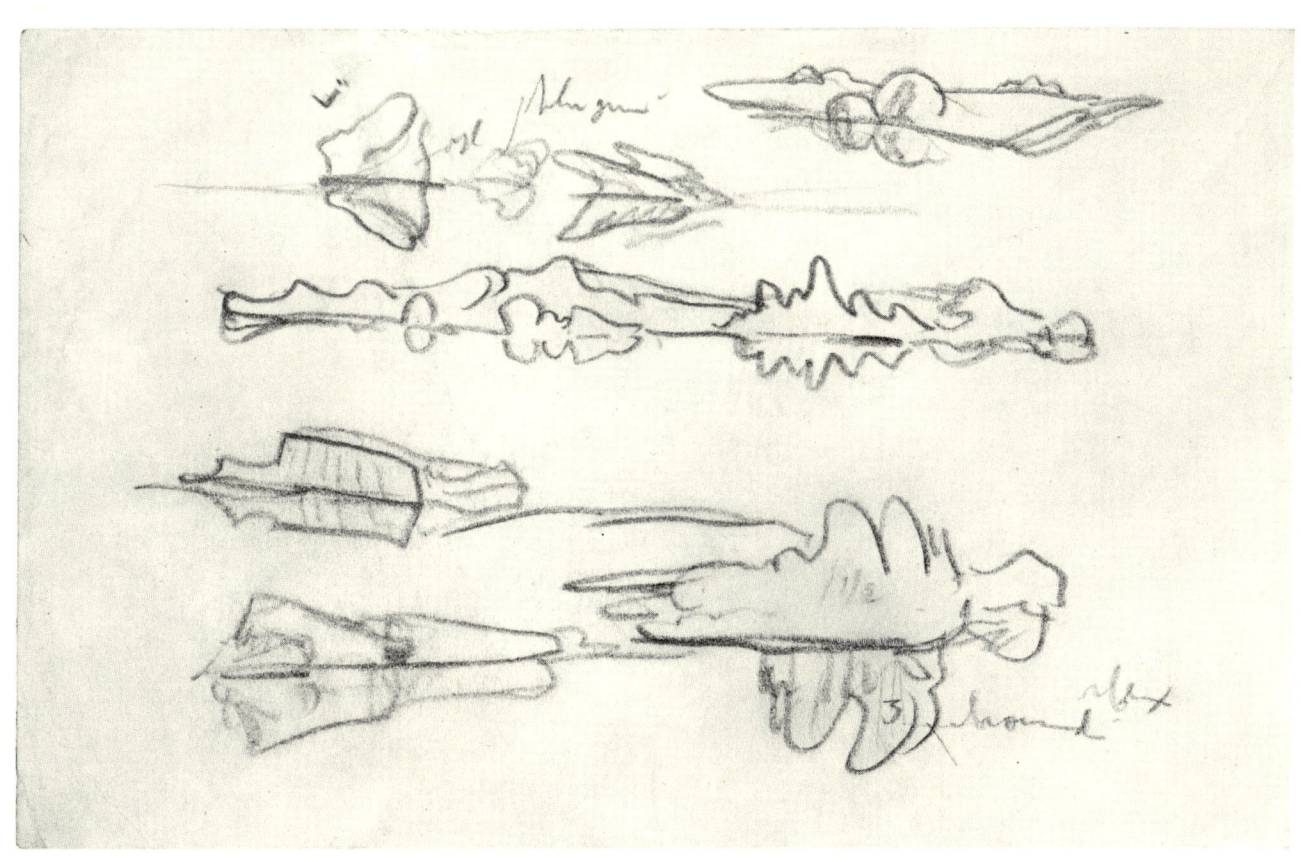

Plate 25 *Old Floe Ice*

Plate 26   *Fram Haven, Ellesmere*

Plate 27   *Fram Haven*

Plate 28 *Cocked Hat Island*

Plate 29 *Cocked Hat Island*

Plate 30 *Bache, Ellesmere Island*

Plate 31 *Bache Post*

Plate 32　*Bache Post*

Plate 33 *Shoreline, possibly Ellesmere Island*

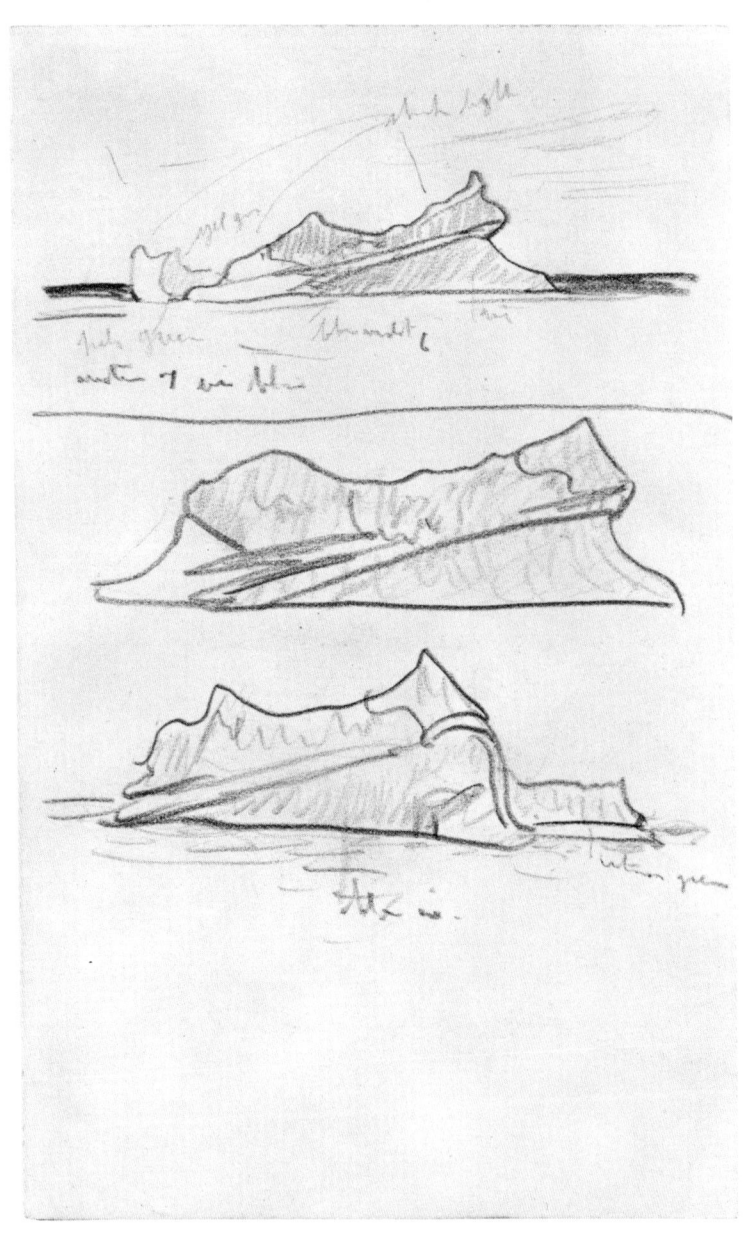

Plate 34
Studies of Three Icebergs

Plate 35   *Ellesmere Island, looking North from Craig Harbour*

Plate 36 *Glacier* on Ellesmere, Rice Straits

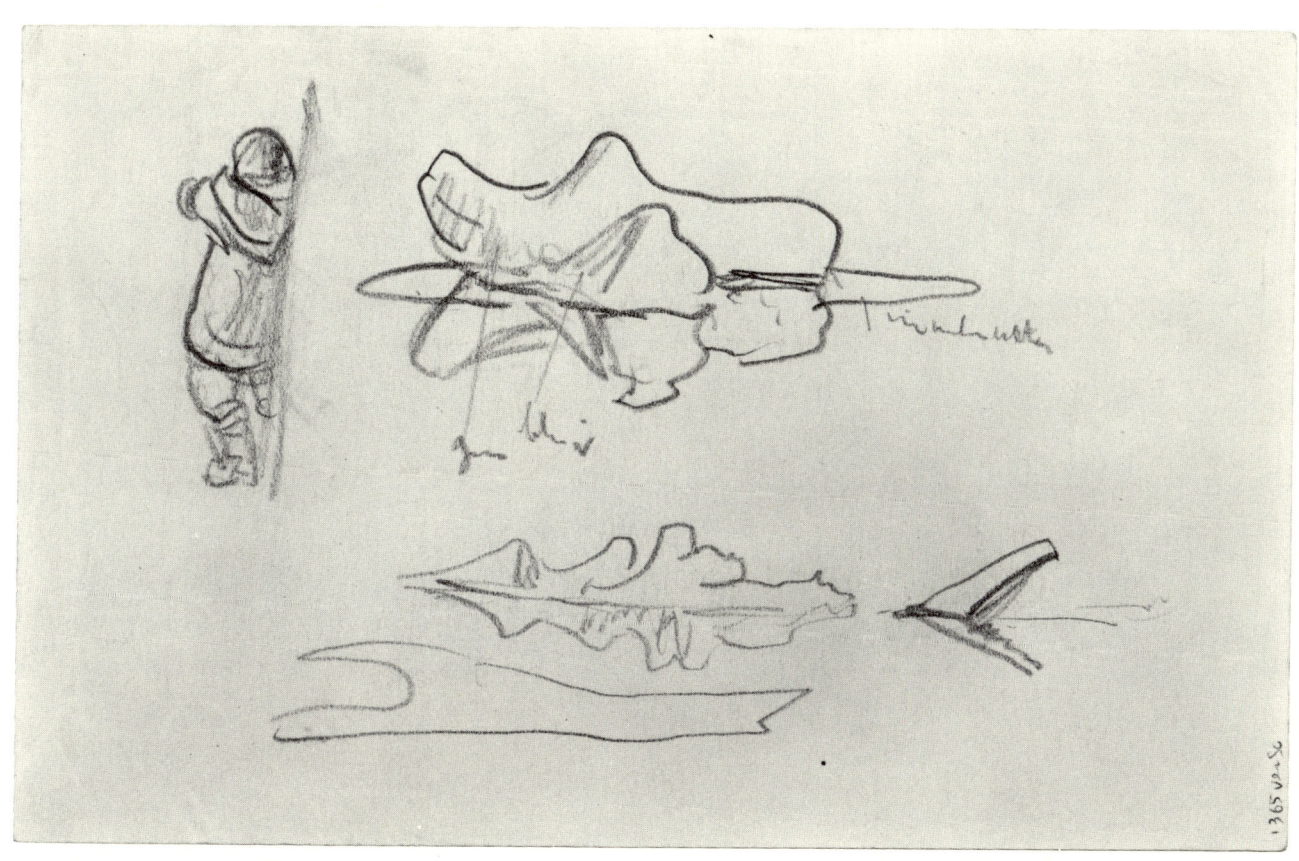

Plate 37 *Ice Studies*

Plate 38 *Sergeant White of the* RCMP, *and* Across from Beechey

Plate 39 *The Mary at Foot of Cliffs, Beechey Island*

Plate 40
Beechey Island

Plate 41 *Beechey Island*

Plate 42 *Ice at Beechey Island*

Plate 43   *Inscription Carved into Stone at Port Leopold, Somerset Island*

Plate 44   *Port Leopold, Somerset Island*

Plate 45   *Thule Eskimo Igloo Ruins, Port Leopold, Somerset Island*

Plate 46 *Admiralty Inlet*

Plate 47   *Admiralty Inlet*

Plate 48 *Arctic Bay*

Plate 49 *Jumping the Ice Floes, Arctic Bay*

Plate 50 *Arctic Bay: Eskimos Crossing the Ice Floes* after Visiting the Beothic

Plate 51   *Studies of Eskimos at Arctic Bay*

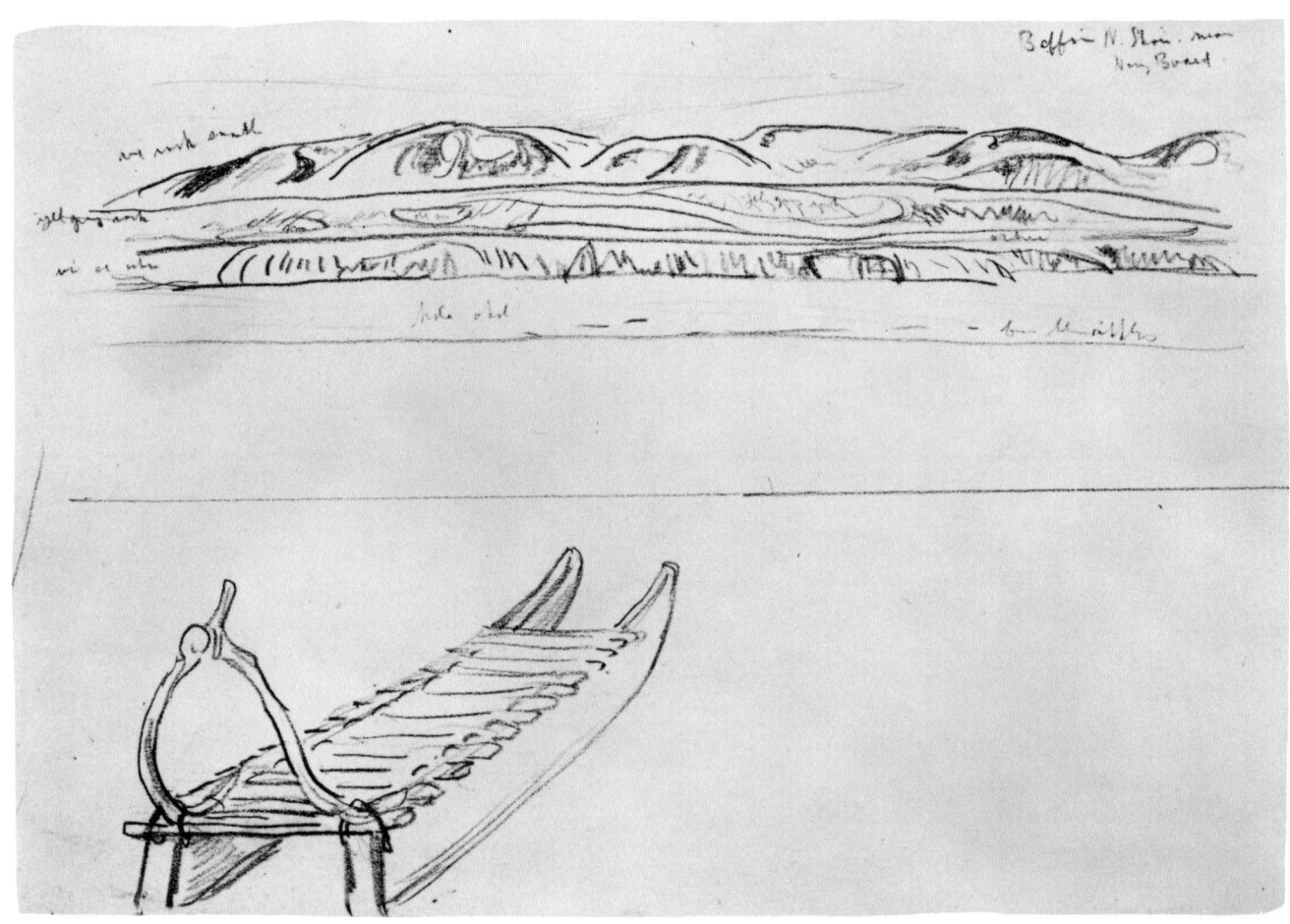

Plate 52 *Baffin, North Shore near Navy Board*

Plate 53
Husky Dogs on Board the Beothic

Plate 54 *South Coast of Bylot Island*

Plate 55   *Pond Inlet*

Plate 56   *Pond Inlet, Baffin Island*

Plate 57   *Pond Inlet, Baffin Shore*

Plate 58 *Pond Inlet, Bylot Island in the Distance*

Plate 59 *Bylot from Pond Inlet*

Plate 60 *Pond Inlet*

Plate 61   *Mt. Morin, Pond's*

Plate 62 *Baffin South of Pond*

Plate 63 *Large Berg*

Plate 64 *North Shore, Cumberland Sound*

Plate 65 *Cumberland Sound*

Plate 66 *Pangnirtung*

Plate 67 *Pangnirtung*

Plate 68 *Pangnirtung*

Plate 69 *Hills of Pangnirtung*

Plate 70
Pyrola, Pangnirtung; Louse Wort and Heather, Lake Harbour

Plate 71
*Studies of Eskimos in Kayaks,
Godhavn and Pangnirtung*

Plate 72
Inuit Figure Studies

Plate 73 *Pangnirtung*

Plate 74 *Entrance to Lake Harbour*

Plate 75 *Lake Harbour*

Plate 76   *Port Burwell*

Plate 77 *Moravian Mission at Port Burwell*

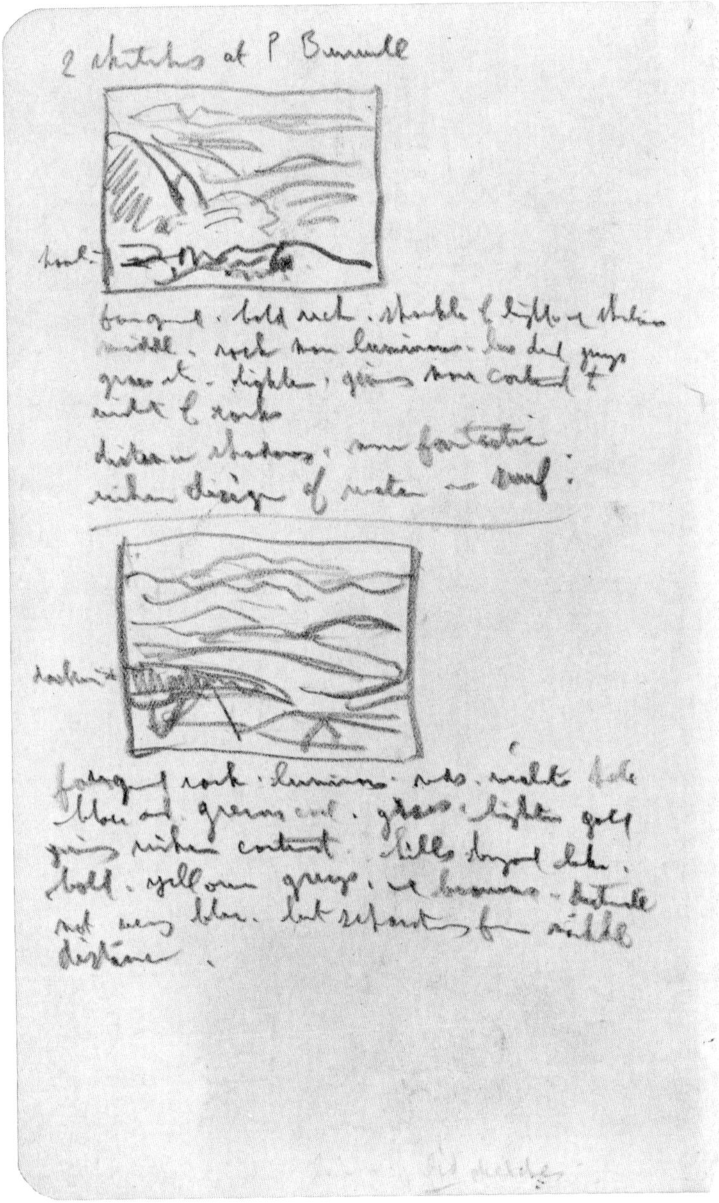

Plate 78
Two Sketches at Port Burwell

Plate 79
Captain Morin

Plate 80   *Portrait Studies on the Beothic,* 1

Plate 81   *Portrait Studies on the Beothic,* II

Plate 82 *On the Hatch of the Beothic*

Plate 83 *Button Islands*

Plate 84 *Cape Chidley*

Plate 85 *Cape Chidley*

Plate 86 *Cape Chidley*

Plate 87 *Cape Chidley*

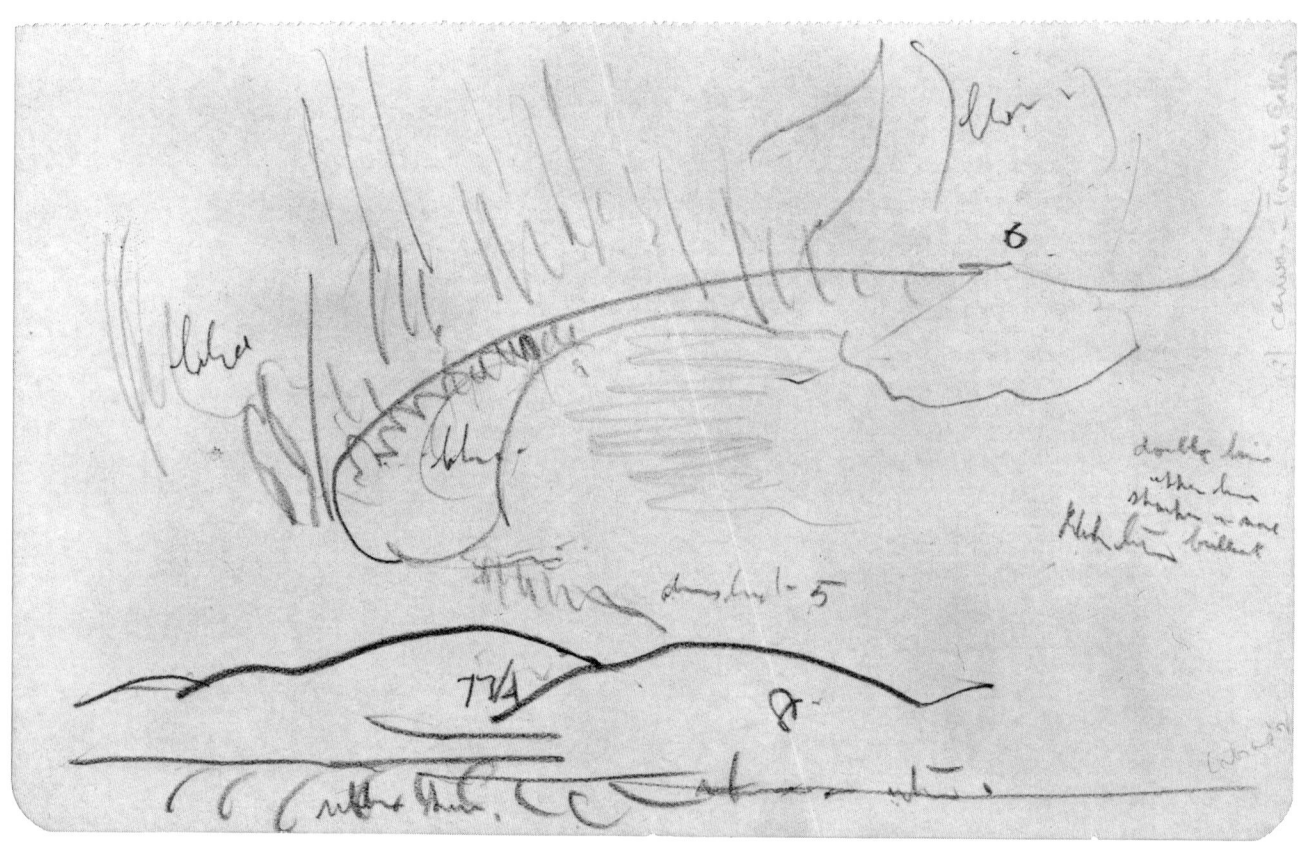

Plate 88 *Aurora Borealis over Labrador*

The Second Diary, 1927 B

Sunday
July 24th

Str. *Beothic*. In Davis Straits. It's Sunday morning, perfectly calm, and the sun faintly shining through a grey sky. Distant ice bergs dot the horizon. Away south you can see the coast of Greenland. We are getting ready to cross to Pond Inlet, Baffin Island. There is speculation about the ice – it goes south on the Baffin side, carried along by the Arctic current; if there is a lot of it, it's hard to push through, but if there is not, it probably means there is a lot hanging round the Bache Peninsula, which will make it worse later for us.

Yesterday morning we slipped out of the fog into Godhavn. How we did it I don't know – there was nothing to go by, neither horn, light or beacon, but we nosed into the snug little harbour, with the frowning snow-covered hills rising behind it, and the heatless sun shining down, about 6 AM. Soon a motor boat came out with the governor of North Greenland in gold braid and such, but beaming all over. The wireless operator, who spoke Oxford English, had no overcoat and wore a straw hat, and tried to look as if he was not half frozen. He said it was the first day there was any excuse to wear a straw hat. We went ashore in one of the ship's boats, the Mounties in their scarlet tunics making a responsive note to all the gay colors of the Eskimo girls. It's an unbelievable village, and you keep pinching yourself to find out if it was a dream or part of the Chauve Souris, or a fairy tale. The Danish houses were quaint and fitted into the rocky landscape, and the Eskimo houses of wood and sods, bits of whale bone and tar paper, just make you laugh. Everybody was laughing, and all in gala attire – such gorgeousness, vermilion top boots or moccasins, fur pants, and jackets of every color, and woolen caps or tuques. It is all rock, rounded like Georgian Bay forms, with grass and wild flowers and pools of water all through it, and dogs, about a dozen to every house, lying all over the place dead to the world. You could almost walk on them and they wouldn't bat an eyelid. Then something would stir the whole outfit, and the howls were like Bedlam let loose. And [then] it would suddenly subside again.

The boys made a movie house with tarpaulin on the deck, and the whole village were invited out to see Felix the Cat and several other films, morning and afternoon performance, wild excitement. There was a Danish artist at Godhavn, he seemed to me like a guy digging lead out of a gold mine, it was rather obvious stuff.

Another artist, Petersen, had been there previously and there were a few fine things left around by him.

Well we can't get away. This morning on the wireless we got Noranda $22.40.

Later: Passing the first floe ice, the Melville Bay pack. It's lovely stuff. Banting said: 'I hope we park somewhere in this kind of stuff.' We were assured that we would find all we wanted. The old *Arctic* was stuck in it once for twenty days. It is chilly, it has been so ever since we left, and you need lots of warm clothes. Lots of flowers at Godhavn, most of them small. I did not recognize them, except the pyrola. The most northerly orchids in the world grow there, I hear.

Monday
July 25th

We followed the edge of the ice pack all yesterday afternoon, looking for a break or a lead they call it. We had to go west a couple of hundred miles to Pond Inlet, our first Canadian port of call. We turned into the ice about 8 PM and are still pushing through it. We have been trying to sketch, but it is very difficult, trying to get a single impression from ice floes that you are passing at six or seven miles an hour. The color is lovely – ice kind of lavender white outside, and opal blue inside, and green under the water. Then the old ship zigzags her way through and you can't find where you left off. This morning the sun came out and it was like spring for a while, but a bank of fog crept up from the south and soon enveloped us, and now we are about at a standstill. Captain Falke has come down from the crows nest, and we may be here all day.

Tuesday
July 26th

Pack opened up enough yesterday to get through, and early this morning we got into open water. Sea quiet, flocks of eider duck and aukpak all around us. A few distant ice bergs. The skies seem minute and far away. Bylot Island is in sight, a line of snow-capped mountains. We should arrive at Pond Inlet about 2 AM and be there about six hours, so we are going to hop right off and get to work. Dr. Malte is also going to rush ashore and grab some specimens. We have terrible appetites and the meals are great. Saw a couple of seals yesterday, we should see more this afternoon.

Later: Pond Inlet is off. We steamed towards the coast all the afternoon, a marvel of a coast, rocky mountains as far as the eye could see, with cloud banks lying thickly over them, so that you could not tell cloud from mountain, only the steep ridges or spines were bare of snow. A long dense bank of fog lay low along the shore line, and made it difficult to find the inlet. As we drew nearer it lifted and we were getting quite excited about getting ashore. The channel seemed to be quite free of ice. The hills on Bylot Island were a golden brown, with here and there red rock showing through. It was a sombre impressive looking country. The channel between Baffin and Bylot is about ten miles across. The Police Post is on the Baffin Id. side. While we were having supper we saw something light across the channel ahead and a few minutes later we bumped into a solid field of ice that made an abrupt line right across the channel. We pushed into it for a hundred feet and stopped dead, twenty miles of solid ice between us and the post. We stopped until midnight, hoping that someone from the post might have come down to the mouth of the channel. They had sent word by radio of our departure, which they might or might not have got. In the meanwhile there were two busy artists rushing round making drawings and sketches. I rushed so hard at the first one, it was a mess and I scraped it out. Seals were flopping in the water all round us. I finished my second sketch at eleven and Banting was just starting another. The hills are sharp pointed, with rocky ridges converging towards the top. It looked more like February than July, the snow did not seem to have melted at all. You could count about fifteen glaciers from the ship, none of them quite reaching the water.

Wednesday
July 27th

We left after midnight and have been following along the coast of Bylot Island. The sea is smooth, a few ice bergs very much eroded are working their way south. You couldn't crowd another peak on to Bylot, there are hundreds and hundreds of them. Some big glaciers, rather flat, sprawl over the foreground, few of them reach the water. In places there appears to be two or three miles of country at the foot of the hills, brownish in color, probably some kind of scant vegetation.

We are now headed for North Devon. Two of the Mounties there are to be relieved. There are three men to a station; they probably haven't seen a soul since last July. The boys we have with us have all been up here before and want to get back. They are a fine lot of chaps. It seems to be the love of adventure that draws them; they are normal, clean-living chaps, none of them with the artistic temperament. Two years ago one of the men at the North Devon post shot himself, probably too temperamental.

Later: Around about 6:30. Little boat put out with the three Mounties. Went ashore, foggy. Esquimos at Police post, swarms of huskies. Dr. Malte made a wild rush with a potato bag and started gathering specimens. From the ship one would think there was no vegetation at all, only a slight bronze color in the lower areas, but when you get into it you find the ground covered with flowers and moss. Heather, poppies, saxifrage, darba, flowering moss, lousewort, etc. Blue flowers seem rare. The barracks seemed cosy. We went into an Esquimo hut, at the side the size of a packing case. The dogs are powerful brutes, but noisy, a dog fight every two minutes. The bay was full of worn out ice, very blue or green – mushroom and other odd forms.

Thursday
July 28th

Went ashore early, fog covered everything, drizzle now and then. Made a sketch and wandered around. It cleared somewhat as we left after lunch. We took the police on board. Had to send an Eskimo back for Banting. Busy afternoon, running along the coast of Devon Island, making drawings as fast as I could go, until fog obscured the receding shores.

Friday
July 29th

Ship rolled a lot in the night, but this morning it is very quiet. We are in Jones Sound, working in to Craig Harbour, to take down the abandoned post and salvage some supplies. Two years ago, Dursh and Sgt. Joy went from here to Dundas Harbour, crossing the sound on the ice and climbing up over North Devon. We are going ashore.

Later: Craig Harbour was full of ice and fog cutting off all the upper half of the landscape. Art is some problem. There is no end of stuff, but everything is moving. the ship, the ice, and then to make it worse, there is nearly always fog hanging round. You have to make a stab at it by either making a drawing or else taking the whole landscape and memorizing the effect. We did not go ashore, it was a mile walk over the ice, and fog at the end of it. We took a quick shot at some young ice bergs, while the steamer was drifting along. It was still for three minutes, but I got a fairly good sketch.

Left for Etah, Greenland after lunch. Sea full of floe ice, with seals dozing, lazing on them. They flop off when the ship gets near. There are whole families of a smaller variety that look funny as they swim, they pop their heads up every few yards. Sometimes only one will come up, then there are four or six or seven all together. Saw three crows or ravens on Ellesmere coast. I believe they stay up here the whole year. Water like glass, and flocks of ducks all over the place, their reflections going along with them.

Saturday July 30th

Everything wonderful but the weather which is vile. The decks were covered with snow this morning when we woke up, and it has been drizzling all day. We are poking our way north through the ice at half speed. Ducks flying all over the place, flocks of small birds called little auks, are bobbing all over the water, bits of seaweed floating round, and walruses waiting on the ice floes for the heat to abate. They undulate themselves into the water as we get near. Made a rotten sketch of an ice berg.

11 PM Etah. We nosed in here out of the fog, god alone knows how, there was nothing to go by, and nothing to see but floating ice. Etah is a well known place, as well known as Hamilton or Trenton. It consists of three tents, one wedge and two made of skins, mostly walrus. There are some broken down ingloos [sic]. The population is variable from none to fifty. At present it is about sixteen and about sixty dogs. We are taking half the population with us to Pond Inlet. They had a rotten winter, a lot of their dogs died of starvation, and the invitation to cross to Pond Inlet was eagerly accepted. The Mounties speak quite a lot of Eskimo and are a tactful lot of boys. Millions of birds round here, flying in big flocks, they are all mixed up in time and are still on the move. Raining hard, good night.

Sunday July 31st

Left Etah at 6.30 AM it cleared before we left, but soon settled down to a steady drizzle with fog. Fortunately there was not much ice. It is one of the worst places in the Arctic. We cut across to Rice Straits. It must be a thrilling place when you can see it – it is only a half mile wide but we ran right into it in the fog. We have two good sailors on the job, Capt. Falke and the ice pilot, Morin. We could just see the base of some tremendous glaciers, and the sea was full of old ice, most fantastic shapes, and the loveliest blues. It is a problem painting ice just by making quick pencil notes in passing. We passed Fram Haven where that good ship wintered. A cross on the top of the rocks is put up in memory of the ship's doctor who died there. We expected the men of the Bache Post to be there, and blew the whistle, but no sign of life. We passed close by Pim Id. where the Greeley expedition spent such a tragic winter, then Cocked Hat Island and on to Bache Peninsula. It is always a question of whether it will be possible to get through the ice in Kane Basin, but we found it clear up to three miles from the Post. It is a strange country, ochre and violet rocks and blue ice. If it was not for the miserable fog that shut off everything above two or three hundred feet. Sgt. Joy and the boys and some Eskimos pushed through the ice in a small boat. Two of our boys are relieving him and another chap. They had to get 20 tons of coal ashore and a lot of other stuff. Fortunately the wind blew the ice out shortly after we arrived. Banting and I went ashore and wandered round in the shale and gravel. Almost nothing growing. We are going to shoot out as soon as the supplies are all ashore. The captain doesn't like this place one bit. We are going to call in at Greenland again. It is green too, compared to this side. 11.30 Banting is still sketching.

Monday August 1st	Caught in the ice. The situation may become very serious within the next few hours. We got about a mile and a half away from Bache Post, and the ice kept getting tighter and the floes larger, and finally the *Beothic* could do nothing. There is open water a mile ahead, but a strong wind has sprung up, and if it drives another ice pack against the one we are in, it may put the *Beothic* out of business. She has a powerful bow – but she is very vulnerable amidships. We are slowly moving with the pack. Later: We got in the lee of an island and most of the ice drifted past us. It opened up enough to push through, and then we raced the thirty miles to Cocked hat Island and got into Rice Straits. Dr. Kane would sure sit up to see a twenty-seven hundred ton steamer plowing through his basin.
Tuesday August 2nd	Snowing and foggy. We are off Craig Harbour somewhere. Nothing to see. The Bache trip was successful, but disappointing for us. The fog enveloped all but the lower hills. There was little vegetation at Bache, it seemed all dried up – mosses, small scrub willow, an odd poppy, and fire weed, but all starved looking. The hills

are architectural, a red and ochre sandstone with very marked lines of stratification.

Have heaps of notes, it's all you have time to get as a rule. We are going to call at Dundas, and then turn westward along the historic Lancaster Sound.

Wednesday August 3rd

Dear Bess. The sun is shining so bright we are all wearing smoked glasses. It cleared up suddenly yesterday after my last paragraph, and it has been bright ever since, even all night. We ran into Craig Harbour, to take away some junk from the abandoned post, so Banting and I got ambitious and climbed a big hill about a thousand feet up, mostly boulders and sharp rocks, covered with moss and lichens. We went onto the next bay, and made a sketch. Got through at 11.30 PM. We were sweltering when we got on top, but we were glad of our coats before we were through. The cold is knife-like up there. We looked over a great stretch of hills and glaciers. The big one at the end of the bay was ten miles wide. Ellesmere Island is a vast ice cap, only bare in spots near the coast. Not a sign of life, not an insect even. We got back to the Post. Sgt. Joy made us some coffee, and it tasted good, too. We got back to the ship about 2 AM, thin ice was forming on the bay. It's a busy life. You have to take the time to work things out for fear of missing something, and you get day and night all mixed up. We find watches almost useless, the time changes so quickly here, and we go east fifty miles one day and a hundred miles west the next. I can't keep up to my notes. Nickel 66. We have a daily paper. We have seven Eskimos, about 15 dogs, a diminishing flock of chickens, two pigs and a cat on board. We are on the way to Dundas, running along the North Devon coast.

Thursday August 4th

All mixed up in the time again. We called in at Dundas Harbour to take an Eskimo family away and leave another in their place, so we got ashore about eight and returned about a quarter to two AM. The sun was shining brightly in the middle of the night. We wandered down the shore accompanied by a number of huskies. They are the friendliest dogs on earth. There was a nice beach so I peeled off, and had a dip. You would have stayed in longer. The light was bright but tinny and hard. I made a rotin [sic] sketch, then we wandered back to the police post, and found Constable Wilson somewhat fuddled but most agreeable. He insisted on making supper for us, and apologized for being too talkative. It is the only time they can celebrate – once a year when the ship comes in. We had cold ham, with excellent bread and canned peaches. Then Wilson insisted on giving Banting a polar bear skin. Well the midnight sun is strange but not very interesting from the standpoint of painting. We are now going west to Beechey Id. where Franklin wintered. We are running parallel with the coast, about three miles out. It is impressive but monotonous red grey sandstone terraces one above the other for a thousand feet, then flattish on top. Every mile or so a glacier comes down and tries to get to the water.

    Later: Not many glaciers after all. We are now at Beechey Id. anchored out in front of it. A desolate looking landscape. A big pile of rock rises about a thousand feet out of the water almost straight up. On the east side it drops down in a series of shale slopes to a bay full of ice. Along the base is a beach of shale, with the hull of a boat lying on it, one of the relief ships left there for him. Beyond and across the bay are the fortress like shores of North Devon Island towering up, with patches of snow still on them. Not a sign of vegetation anywhere. Raining and foggy, and a big sea running. We cannot go on until it clears, as compasses are almost useless here on account of proximity to the magnetic pole. Dogs are giving a concert, a general protest against iron decks and rain, and the doggone country generally.

Friday August 5th

Storm bound at Beechey Island. We can't get ashore. There is a lot of floe ice hanging round and we have had to change our anchorage twice, and they don't want to risk a small boat out. It has been foggy too, and color cheese [sic] and the water here is much greener than it was Kane Basin way. It takes the distinction out of your composition. The ice is less colorful too. This is all because I made a punk sketch which I scraped off. No more ice bergs down this way. The islands are not so large or so high and there are no more big glaciers. But there is lots of floe ice that bobs up from somewhere whenever there is a wind to shove it.

    Later: Fog obscured everything.

Saturday August 6th

Bright and sunny. Closed in by floe ice which extends as far as we can see. We went ashore. I made two drawings. There is the hull of a schooner on the beach and a lot of debris – rusty tins and barrel staves mostly. There is the remains of the winter quarters which Franklin and five years later Belcher probably used. It was all torn down some years ago by a bird named Janes, who was later murdered by Eskimos. They did not do it soon enough. There is a memorial erected by McClintock, a wooden post and a marble slab. Wood lasts indefinitely up here. There are a lot of water barrels, thirty or forty of them, that could be used today. Some of them have been gnawed up by bears. They have been there about eighty years. We took out a paper that Capt. Bernier left in a whiskey bottle in 1922 and put our little names in. The bottle was still very pungent. We are here until the ice moves.

Later: Fog, and ice as far as one can see into the fog. It keeps the crew busy, as the big floes shove us in towards shore, drag the anchors as though they were mere watch fobs, and we have to start the engines and pound through it, or climb up on it and bust it with our weight, then back up and run into it again until we get into an open space, then anchor until another mess comes on. We cannot leave the harbour because harbours are scarce, and this is a good one. Evening dog concert on, about thirty of them howling like wolves.

Sunday
August 7th

We are poking round Lancaster Sound in a dense fog, ice fields all round. We don't know what to do. We cannot navigate west of here unless it clears up. We are probably here two weeks too early. Summer doesn't start here until about August 25th. Winter starts about August 15th, so it takes some figuring. Anyway the captain got anxious about staying in Beechey. A storm could have piled us ashore with the ice. I expect we will drift around here for a couple of days and then give up the idea of reaching Melville.

Monday
August 8th

Port Leopold, Somerset Island. Could not get through the ice to Cornwallis, so turned south to Somerset. It was foggy all night and up till noon, but it cleared up and we got in here. It is a H.B. Post which is probably closing up. We are waiting instructions by wireless. It's a pale yellow ochre country with little to seize on in the way of form. It appears to have no vegetation at all, but possibly when we go ashore we will find a little saxifrage, moss, etc.

The chaps from the post with several Eskimos have just come on board. I should not think they would be sorry to leave. It seems nothing but an endless stretch of yellowish shale, with ridges of sedimentary rock coming out on the hillsides.

Later: Went ashore. H.B. Post and a few half breeds in wedge tents, nothing picturesque in the least. They all wore supplied clothing. The landscape is just an endless pile of sharp stones, not even moss or lichen to soften it. Cold fog banks lay on all the hills, raw chilling stuff, it blew down on us frequently and ruined what poor prospects there were of making a sketch. James Ross wintered here in 1848-49. There is an initial cut in a boulder on the shore. E.I. 1849. Dr. Malte tells me the southern end of Somerset is very rich in flora, but he could only find ten species today. I don't know what animals live on, have not seen any land animals yet, not even bears. We don't get much time ashore.

Tuesday
August 9th

Low down fog shutting off everything over a hundred feet up. We went ashore in the motor boat. Swarms of birds, sea pigeon, gulls, and a kind of wicked looking cuss, gull shaped but black and with his legs trailing behind in flight. New job: archeology. Nothing to sketch so we dug out some old ingloos. The guy whose house I picked on must have been part Scotch, he left so little. We got some pieces of bone, spear heads, knife handles etc. Whale bone and walrus ribs were scattered all over the place. There are remains of ingloos everywhere it was possible to hunt and get shelter, all the way to the north of Ellesmere. Haven't made a sketch for four days. I think the Melville Island trip is going to be abandoned. I don't think the country to the west is as paintable as the east, so it will give us a little more time on Baffin Island.

Wednesday
August 10th

The friendly Arctic — rain, wind and fog. I have been making a drawing of an ingloo, stones and bones. I have quite a collection of pen drawings. There is more to draw than to paint, or it is more possible to draw, as everything is on the move. We are still anchored in Port Leopold, waiting for a wireless message as to whether we take the H.B. outfit on board. Over a month since I left Toronto. I hope you are having a better summer than we are. This whole country is at its best in the early spring, clear and bright, but of course below zero, and it would be difficult to get notes. None of the police boys say much about the cold. After reading Dr. Kane one gets the impression that it is a fight to exist. Sgt. Joy travelled over 1500 miles early this year, across Ellesmere to Ringes, North Cornwallis, Graham and back to Ellesmere. He was rather peeved about being relieved, as he had another trip in contemplation. He is a remarkable individual, not scientifically trained, but very observant, and I imagine as fine an explorer as any one who has been up here.

|Thursday August 11th|

Rain and fog. We are on our way to Arctic Bay. We took on twelve more people and more dogs and expect to pick up a few more in Arctic Bay. I don't find that H.B. people are very popular. The steward expressed the general opinion in saying: they give nothing, but expect everything. Capt. Morin has been giving me some sidelights on the Janes murder which took place at Cape Crawford about five years ago. It blew a gale all yesterday afternoon and evening, and we were lucky to be in harbour. The bay filled up with ice that had been pounded to bits outside, however the wind could not blow the fog off the hills. I made one sketch from notes. All this country is sedimentary rock, flat topped, and long ridges of strata protruding through its own debris. From now on it should be more exciting – pointed hills, sharp peaks with glaciers all over them. Nunataks sticking out – that is what they call isolated peaks that rise above the surrounding ice.

We don't get any exercise. There is very little deck room, we are all piled up with dories, motor boats, kayaks, sleighs, a small flotilla. Then on the few occasions we get ashore we want to paint and draw all the time, so don't expect to see a big weather-beaten brute. Noranda 21.40. Our news is mostly about the prince at the Baldwins, with an odd murder thrown in. We have no radio, only wireless. The radio up here is almost useless in the summer months but quite clear in the winter. We have been getting messages for the *Stanley* down in Hudson Bay and relaying them on. Hudson Bay is very hard to reach by wireless.

Friday August 12th

Dear dear. One is an exclamation and the other you. I'm still full of sleep. Went ashore at three AM, wandered with Banting over a stretch of old glacial moraines. Made a sketch and wandered back along the beach. Shelves of sand or gravel, and further back boulders. Traces of Eskimo occupation, rings of boulders for tents, and places where slabs of flat rock had been arranged for sleeping on. Further down the shore met a H.B. man, with a troop of Eskimos walking along the beach to get beyond the ice and visit the steamer. They all stepped up and shook hands with me very genially – the big chief, three or four other men, a lot of kids, tattooed ladies and the village belles. Smiling is their chief means of communication with us. I felt like the Prince of Wales. Our boat came over and [I] not having high boots, an Eskimo carried me out on his back. I assisted the ladies on board. They smell rather high — smiling at about six feet is as intimate as I would care to get. This is Arctic Bay, Baffin Land North. We arrived about midnight. There was a slight impression of night, and a sunset, all rosy red on the gothic cliffs of Admiralty Inlet. Miles of big cathedrals and Hart Houses violet, red and orange. Closer to the shore you could see vegetation. Sgt. Joy told me he traveled along the plateau from Port Leopold to Admiralty Inlet over a hundred miles, and scarcely a blade of grass the whole way. A couple of years ago fifteen Eskimos died of starvation further down the inlet, while round here they had so much food they were throwing it away. The Eskimos were presented with Confederation medals. Some future archeologist will dig them up in the igloos. I fell asleep and did not see the ceremony.

Saturday
August 13th

Sun shining and the sea like glass. We are running along the coast of Bylot for a second attempt to get into Pond Inlet. We were to get in by the western passage this morning, but found it still frozen over. We keep on accumulating Eskimos and dogs. The fore deck is piled up with motor boats, sleighs, dogs and props. Fighting and howling goes on all day long. The Eskimos' state rooms are down the hold on top of the coal, and they think it pretty swell. We stopped to pick up one family yesterday at Arctic Bay. They came hopping over the ice floes to the steamer. They wanted to go to Pond Inlet, a couple of hundred miles further on. I think their only reason for moving was the desire for a ride on the big smoke-belching ship. They are a scream at times. The bay filled up with ice and we could not use the boats. The whole population from babies to grandmas came jumping over the ice to see us off. They were terribly disappointed when they found it was too late to come aboard. Eliza crossing the ice was nothing to their departure for the shore a mile away — about thirty of them, with dogs, in a Chauve Souris medley of costumes. They trade them awful junk at the H.B. — old print dresses of twenty years ago, skirts down to their ankles, red blue pink, seal skin pants, the loose Arctic shirt with the bag at the back for the papoose, old army tunics, and every cap imaginable. And all hopping from one chunk of ice to another, throwing their dogs across the wide spaces. Old girls who you would hardly think could would hardly think could walk, jumping like two year olds and four year old kids following them. one old girl had a youngster on her shoulders with his legs tight round her neck. if the space was too wide, they jumped on a smaller piece and gave it a shove with one foot as they stepped on. as a show it was a marvel.

We hope to get to Ponds Inlet late to-night. from accounts it is interesting. Talking t Sgt Joy, he regrets having to leave very much. he wanted to go round the north coast of Ellesmere and in to Lake Hazen. he thinks very little of Canadian Arctic expeditions. merely trips to places already well enough known. expensive and purposeless. Bernier has a poor reputation among Arctic explorers. he is less an explorer than an exploiter. we have a white boy who came aboard yesterday. a son of Caron one of Bernier's officers who married an Eskimo girl, raised a family. went back to Quebec and got really married by the church to a French girl. then fell overboard from the Arctic one night when he was pickled. thats that. Mackenzie our chief is a good Canadian, straight as they make them. they could not have found a better man. most of his life has been spent in the Yukon and he is a big pleasant active chap. he makes me think of Mr Williams.

Monday Aug 15th. Just starting in to write when this bird bore down on us and made us haul of our anchors in a hurry and get out of his way. he ran aground fifty just from us at the eye on him. Its a cots is shucking his long time since I write in this. we

got in to Pond Inlet Saturday Night. there was a full moon running along the ridge back of the settlement. seemed to be rolling along the tob of it. There's so much

walk, jumping like two-year olds, and five-year old kids following them. One old girl had a youngster on her shoulders with his legs tight round her neck. If the space was too wide, they jumped on a smaller piece and gave it a shove with one foot as they stepped on. As a show it was a marvel.

We hope to get to Pond Inlet late tonight. From accounts it is interesting. Talking to Sgt. Joy, he regrets having to leave very much. He wanted to go round the northern coast of Ellesmere, and in to Lake Hazen. He thinks very little of Canada's Arctic expeditions, merely trips to places already well known, expensive, and purposeless. Bernier has a poor reputation among Arctic explorers, he is less an explorer than an exploiter. We have a white boy who came aboard yesterday, a son of Caron, one of Bernier's officers, who married an Eskimo girl, raised a family, went back to Quebec and got really married by the Church to a French girl, then fell overboard from the *Arctic* one night when he was pickled, and that's that.

MacKenzie, our chief, is a good Canadian, straight as they make them, they could not have found a better man. Most of his life has been spent in the Yukon and he is a big, pleasant, active chap. He makes me think of Mr. Williams.

Monday
August 15th

Just starting in to write when this bird bore down on us and made us haul up our anchors in a hurry and get out of his way. He ran aground fifty feet from us and the Cap is keeping his eye on him. It's a long time since I wrote in this. We got in to Pond Inlet Saturday night. There was a full moon running along the ridge back of the settlement, seemed to be rolling along the top of it. There is so much going on, it's like a three ring circus and you can't follow it all. Went ashore Sunday morning – glorious sunshine. There is a big stretch of low country, rolling hills covered with grass, moss and flowers, numerous streams running through and ponds of shallow water in about every dip. In the background in all directions were mountains shooting up. There was too much to sketch – you wanted to explore. I had one of your chocolate bars, so wandered all day, came back to the shore and went to the remains of an old Eskimo settlement, and then went along to the Police Barracks, and Corporal Pettie cooked me a real supper. I stayed the night with them. Dr. Banting was already there. Two of the boys were moving south and were much disgusted. South I found was Pangnirtung. They all want to go to Bache, the country Dr. Kane anguishes over. There are about fifty or sixty Eskimos round here, a cheerful, smiling lot. Houses made of bits of everything, and surrounded by dogs, about twenty round every house. They howl and fight and swarm all over the place, but don't bother us in the least. About half a dozen will follow you out sketching, and look bored and clear off when you start to sketch. Today it was foggy and rainy again, and nothing to do. It's hard when time is so limited. Not much bird life. A big raven was circling round me yesterday while I was sketching. There are not many small birds, snow buntings and a smaller bird similar in appearance. Bon soir.

Wednesday August 17th	We left for home last night, and are now proceeding south about fifteen miles out from the Baffin Land coast. The sun is shining and the sea is smooth. We had quite a time getting supplies off at Pond Inlet, the ice fairly packed the channel and the steamer would have to pull out and hunt for open water. We spent most of yesterday avoiding ice. About four PM it eased up a little and we got back to the post, and got ashore long enough to make a sketch. I could spend a couple of months happily at Pond Inlet, it's a great sketching ground. there are a lot of lakes in a few miles, and country easy to run over. However the Cap was in a hurry to get out. The ice situation gave him no rest, so now we are on our way to Clyde, Pangnirtung, Lake Harbour, Port Burwell and Sydney. We picked up Dr. Livingstone at Pond, he had gone there by dog team from Pangnirtung. We left three Mounties, and took the three from there with us. The sketches are coming slowly, have about two dozen and hope to make it forty. It is not an ideal way to work, you see all kinds of things you just cannot do while you are moving.... 　　It's night and the moon is shining – a strange moon cut sharp in half, and reflecting in the streaks of water between the ice. Further north there is a mirage. The ice bergs on the horizon are floating in the sky. We just ran up on deck to see two polar bears out on the ice, quite a way off, like two daubs of clotted cream. On the other side very sharp snow-covered peaks of Baffin Land. It's a great life.
Thursday August 18th	Another day gone and art just where it was. We shoved our way into Clyde through miles of ice to leave some Eskimos and their dogs there. It was a lovely cloudless day, but not a wildly exciting place, and a bad place to be if the wind should tighten the ice up. We went ashore and were in the middle of a sketch when the whistle

blew and we had to hurry back to the beach. And we are now pushing ice again on the way to Pangnirtung. Saw some ptarmigan and a very large raven. Clyde used to be great caribou country, but caribou are being exterminated all over the Arctic. The Eskimo takes no thought for the morrow, he kills everything whether he needs it or not, and then starves himself out. We have been living on fresh salmon lately. They come in towards the shore to get up to the lakes where they winter. There are very few other fish. There is sea weed scattered along the beaches, not in great quantities or very large forms, but it seems to grow nearly everywhere. The walrus feed on it to some extent. No news of Noranda for a week. We are not a literary aggregation. I don't think anyone on board ever heard of Blake. The Captain has read a great deal about Arctic exploration, so has Mr. MacKenzie and Sgt. Joy, but the rest just read to find out what happens. Malte is a marvellous booze artist and I should think a very able botanist. In spite of his Falstaffian girth he loses no opportunity of hunting for specimens. He can't bend over very well so he lies down and pokes round the ground with a microscope. Dr. Livingstone travelled over two thousand miles by dog team since he left the ship last year. He is a picturesque cuss. We should have a portrait man with us. Some of the Eskimos are very fine too, much more paintable than Injuns, and much more likable.

Friday August 19th   Not much of a day, only the boundless waste, cold and foggy, and everyone asleep. I read a French book about a T.B. Sanatorium, morbid stuff. Tonight we passed close to an immense iceberg. The fog has lifted, the northern sky is sunset, the southern sky night with a little piece of moon left and Jupiter blazing bright, and distant icebergs gleaming coldly.

Saturday August 20th   Nothing but water and the distant peaks of Baffin Land. The ship is rolling, and no one on deck. I have just finished Jorn Uhl. You gave it to me long ago, it's fine – sentimental and a little too much preaching, but it's robust and human. Well, we hope to finish up strong at Pangnirtung, and perhaps Lake Harbour, but it does not sound very exciting. I imagine Port Burwell will be good, but our stay short. There are of course far more natives in the south. They like living with white men; they feel a sense of security. So does the white man with the Eskimo. But some of the Mounties will tell you quite frankly that the best thing we can do for the Eskimo is to get out and let him live in his own way. We get him accustomed to luxuries – tea, sugar, jam, etc. which he is very fond of. To get these things he has to find fox skins and neglect his own hunting of seals, walrus, narwhal etc., and often starves to death. It is fox skins that bring the white men up here and from what you gather it is a pretty shifty business. From Arctic Harbour alone the H.B. Company loaded 2,000 fox skins on the *Beothic* – worth a hundred thousand dollars, and the natives have nothing but a few tents, and clothes that the Salvation Army wouldn't take as a gift, when they should be clothed in furs and have everything for their simple needs. The police are doing a lot for them, getting them to look a little further ahead and to be less wasteful. They don't think much of missionaries, it's the beginning of the end when they arrive. Greenland has pretty well solved the native problem, but it will be impossible for us to do it the same way.

Sunday August 21st	Going up Cumberland Sound. Rather misty in spots, but sun shining. Big undulating hills with steep shores. Got into Pangnirtung after supper. Jenkins, the parson, came out in a kayak, paddling a little nervously – they are difficult to handle. Weeks and Haycock, the geologists whom we were to pick up, are still away. Went ashore, made a punk sketch. But the country looks interesting.
Monday August 22nd	We prepared for a big day, and woke up to find rain and fog. Made some pencil drawings of Eskimo dwellings, and then went up the hill back of the settlement, and wandered round most of the day in the drizzle. Rich foregrounds – moss and lichens and big boulders, but above us the curtain of fog shutting everything off. Weeks and Haycock had returned about midnight. They had caught a wireless message from us four days previous and had been on the go ever since, to arrive in time. Well, we kept going in the drizzle, dined on some Bess Housser chocolate and returned empty-handed to the police post, and had supper. All the Eskimos went out to the steamer and saw a movie show down in the coal hole. They whooped when they saw themselves, taken on a previous trip, and at Felix the Cat, and at some flappers in bathing suits on the beach in Vancouver. It makes you realize right away too the value of simplicity.

Well, there is only Lake Harbour now, in which to find the great Arctic landscape. We are getting south, the snow only lies on the tops of the hills, the poppies cannot stand the warmth and languish in their southern climes. A lot of other flowers have given up too, or gone higher up on the hills.

Tuesday
August 23rd

Drizzle and fog. Went out of Cumberland Sound without seeing it, only a faint vista of land through the mist.

Wednesday
August 24th

Dreamed that you and Fred and I with a bunch of Germans were away out on the ice, which was very unsafe, and the land a long way off. We are in Hudson Straits, and it is dark, foggy, windy and raining. It has been a slow day. I made a sketch from notes, and a pen drawing, and washed a shirt and oiled my boots. The Cap hasn't much faith in the Hudson Bay route, and he was born inside the Arctic Circle and had to push through ice half his life, and has not much love for it. Bon soir.

Thursday
August 25th

Arrived at Lake Harbour in the afternoon. It is an exciting place, like parts of Lake Superior, rocky islands all along the coast, lots of color in the rocks. We went ashore – grey miserable weather as usual. Little lakes all over the place. Sub-arctic vegetation, quite a lot of soil, and a rich carpet of flowers and moss, even buttercups and dandelions, and willow bushes a couple of feet high.

Friday
August 26th

Raining when we got up but it stopped and we went ashore. The boys are working like Trojans on their new post. In the past they have patrolled down here from Pangnirtung. We went back country over three miles. It's a marvel of a place, full of rhythms, you would love it. I was talking to you all day about it. It is old caribou country, but all that is left of the caribou are a few mouldering bones and horns. The Eskimo killed everything when we gave him firearms. The rocks are full of mica, you can pick up big chunks of it. There is a lake every five minutes. There are big gravel stretches smooth as tennis courts, only all big curves. Some of them run up four or five hundred feet, and on top you will find boulders of different stones altogether, lying on top of it, but not embedded at all.

There was not a glimmer of joy in the weather, it looked sore because it was short of rain. We dined as usual on Bess Housser chocolate. The blue berries are in blossom, and there is the bear berry, not quite ripe and not very exciting. Not much sign of life; lots of lemming holes but we haven't seen one of the owners yet. We have to make an extra stop, Wakeham Bay on the south side of Hudson Straits. Cheerio.

Saturday
August 27th

Had a great day. Went ashore, the sun was shining, lasted an hour. We explored to the west, found a lake every three minutes. About noon we climbed a big ridge, with little lakes all over it, almost to the top. It was so windy we could hardly face it. It sloped down steeply on the other side, to a big valley, about three miles across to another ridge, and below, lakes as far as you could see, often just little ridges of rock or meadow separating one from another. Lots of flowers – fire weed, pyrola, saxifrage, arctic cotton, but little sign of life. Scared up a rabbit, a big white fellow with dabs of black on him.

 Ate the last of your chocolate and some biscuits for lunch. Made three sketches, though it had turned miserably grey. Got back to the shore and had quite a time attracting the ship's attention. Eventually made a fire from some old stuff the H.B. people had left on the shore.

Sunday
August 28th

On the way to Wakeham Bay, crossing Hudson Straits. The sun shone this morning, and everything seemed to delay us getting ashore. They had been working very hard at the new barracks, and so Sunday they all slept in. We got ashore, and it seemed so strange to have sunlight I could not find anything to do. We went tearing all over the place. I have been looking for something that I visualized – it exists round here, but I did not discover it. An arctic landscape, no place in particular, a generalized landscape.... I got on a big hill that looked over miles of hills and lakes, and of course made a punk sketch.

 We left Paul Dursh and Sgt. White at the post, and left about three PM. Nearing the end of our trip. We may be in Sydney next Sunday. It will be great to hear from you.

Monday
August 29th

It's a pitch black night and we are going half speed for fear of ice bergs. We are heading for Cape Chidley, we round it for Burwell, our last stop before Sydney. This morning I woke up to the sound of the anchor chains rattling. We were in Wakeham Bay, a pastoral looking landscape, grassy slopes and big round hills, and a Revellion Freres and H.B. post, and an airplane base under construction, and the *Stanley* and the *Larch* anchored near us, quite a metropolis. We went ashore a short time. The air station will be here for sixteen months, studying ice conditions in Hudson Straits. Another post is being established at Nottingham Island, and the third one yet to be near Burwell.

Had quite a talk with Major Lawrence, who is in charge, a good clean-cut boy. His team mate Carr Harris looked like a young daredevil. Their expedition ... [NOTE: unfortunately, A.Y.'s page 24 is missing. It would be the last of August 29, August 30 (at Port Burwell) and the beginning of August 31. His page 25 follows.] ...

Wednesday
August 31st

lying in crevasses. A few Eskimo living in tents. They are the vanishing race, too much contact with white people is the end of them.

South Baffin Land looks like a mild gentle country compared with this, looking across the miles of rocky ridges and the sea breaking along the miles of granite coast. I saw a little grave stone, erected over Solomon Lane, who arrived in June when the flowers were impatiently pushing through the departing snows. He went away three months later in September when the flowers were dried or frozen up and the snow was sweeping over Ungava again.

Well we are on the way to Sydney. Last night the aurora made great spirals in the sky, while the Eskimo were down in the hold seeing the movie show. It was cold, the pools in the rocks were ice covered this morning, but the sun is shining and the sea sparkling and it's all good.

Thursday
September 1st

Well, we got a shaking up. You couldn't stand up without hanging on to something. Everything in the cabin was sliding back and forth – trunks, valises, boots, and us. However we ran in the lee of the Button Islands, and it got quieter. We passed Cape Chidley, a bold headland, the northerly point of Labrador. Snow still lying in patches. From there south it was a great line of mighty forms, an heroic looking country, that does not even blink when the Atlantic hurls icebergs at it.

Today it is quiet, no land in sight. I made two sketches from notes made at Burwell. We heard about the Germans winning the swimming race, in the most anti-German burg in Canada, wasn't it lovely. The Bon Dieu has a sense of humor, letting a little kid lick all the champions when he was just nobody, and then letting a Fritzie get away with Toronto's $50000 [sic]. If he would do everything that way I would go to church on Sundays.

But six weeks ago we were rushing out on deck every time we passed an iceberg. Now we are too blasé to look out of the port hole at a dozen of them. [NOTE: there is no entry for September 2nd]

Saturday
September 3rd

In the gulf, dark and foggy, the old whistle is blowing every few minutes. We are getting to inhabited parts – we seldom blew it up north. The only thing you were likely to hit were icebergs. Yesterday the sun shone all day long, and for the first time this summer we were on deck in our shirt sleeves. Tomorrow night we should be in Sydney. Today we are packing up. I am afraid a lot of this sounds too much like a diary and you will get sleepy over it. It is hard not to be a tourist when you are travelling like one and have everything done for you.

Strange, we have been voyaging in one of the most romantic countries in the world and yet nearly everyone on the expedition has been taking the artificial stimulus of detective stories to while away the time. I would like a couple of weeks, paddling, swimming and chopping wood on the Georgian Bay, to get the old muscles in shape. An occasional scramble over rocks is all I have had in the way of exercise.

We have been a very happy party, all very genial. There have been only two gentlemen below par. The chief steward is our bootlegger and I suspect a crook at times, and the other was a big hunk of a Mountie who was always trying to put things over. He was as sensitive as a rhinoceros. He was snooping round for tobacco one day and hit up Banting: 'Hey, doc, are you the guy that has the Edgeworth?' Fortunately he stayed at Pangnirtung, and the whole ship is snikkering [sic] On leaving he sold the chief steward a white fox skin. It was a large rabbit with a fox's tail and head stuck on. Everyone knows except the foxy steward. I gave the flash lamp to one of the boys at Lake Harbour who will be there for the long night. I still have a lot of medical supplies. Some of them were very useful, just the same ... The great want of the Eskimo, they tell us, is chewing gum. Good night.

Sunday

Hit Sydney 11 PM.

List of Drawings

All drawings, including those in private collections, are coded for purposes of identification.

Plate 1 *The Beothic at Sydney, Nova Scotia*
5 x 8 inches; before sailing on July 16, 1927; private collection (njg 70)

Plate 2 *The Beothic, Sydney,* N.S.
5 x 8; July 16; private (njg 71)

Plate 3 *The Beothic at Sydney,* N.S.
5 x 8; July 16; private (njg 72)

Plate 4 *The Stern of the Beothic*
5 x 8; July 16; private (njg 73)

Plate 5 *First Icebergs, Belle Isle*
9 x 5½; July 18; private (njg 80 verso)

Plate 6 *Icebergs and Mirage*
5½ x 9; July; private (njg 88)

Plate 7 *Four Icebergs*
9 x 5½; July; private (njg 84)

Plate 8 *Icebergs on Skyline near Godhavn, Greenland*
5 x 8; July 24; private (njg 100)

Plate 9 *Icebergs at Godhavn*
5½ x 9; July 23; Firestone Art Collection, Ottawa (f 34)

Plate 10 *Godhavn, Eskimo House*
5½ x 9; July 23; private (njg 97)

Plate 11 *Dark House in Godhavn*
5½ x 9; July 23; private, Denmark (njg 96)

Plate 12 *Pushing Through Melville Pack Ice*
5 x 8; July 25; private (njg 1692)

Plate 13 *Towards Pond Inlet, Ice and Fog*
5 x 8; July 25; private (njg 1693)

Plate 14 *Mirage*
5½ x 9; July; private (njg 89 verso)

Plate 15 *Bylot near Pond Inlet*
5½ x 9; July; private (njg 1665)

Plate 16 *Baffin North of Pond*
5½ x 9; 1927 (later dated incorrectly as 1930); Firestone Art Collection, Ottawa (f 67)

Plate 17 *Above Pond Inlet, Baffin*
5½ x 9; July; private (njg 1678)

Plate 18 *Dundas Harbor, July 27th*
7½ x 11¼; July 27; National Gallery of Canada, gift of A.Y. Jackson (NGC 17692/njg 2079)

Plate 19 *Arctic Plants, North Devon Island*
9 x 5 ½; likely July 27; later dated incorrectly as 1930; Firestone Art Collection (f 79)

Plate 20 *Coburg Island*
7 ½ x 10 ⅞; July 28; Norman Mackenzie Art Gallery, Regina, gift of the Artist (njg 755 recto)

Plate 21 *North Devon Island*
7 ½ x 11; July 28; National Gallery of Canada (NGC 17724/ njg 186)

Plate 22 *Etah, Greenland*
5 x 8; July 30; private (njg 105)

Plate 23 *Flower Studies, Etah, Greenland*
5 ⅞ x 5 ½; likely July 30; private (njg 107)

Plate 24 *Etah, Greenland, summer camp*
5 x 8; July; Norman Mackenzie Art Gallery, Regina, gift of the Artist; used for Plate 4 in *The Far North* (njg 752)

Plate 25 *Old Floe Ice*
5 x 8; July; private (njg 185)

Plate 26 *Fram Haven, Ellesmere*
5 x 8; July 31; private; used for Plate 5 in *The Far North* (njg 216)

Plate 27 *Fram Haven*
5 x 8; July; private (njg 1658)

Plate 28 *Cocked Hat Island*
5 ½ x 9; July 31; private; compare to Plate 6 in *The Far North* (njg 1662)

Plate 29 *Cocked Hat Island*
5 ½ x 9; July 31; with 1930 added later, incorrectly; private (njg 1664 recto)

Plate 30 *Bache, Ellesmere Island*
5 x 8; likely July 31; private (njg 1669)

Plate 31 *Bache Post*
5 x 8; likely July 31; Norman Mackenzie Art Gallery, gift of the Artist; used for Plate 7 of *The Far North* (njg 753)

Plate 32 *Bache Post*
5 ½ x 9; July; Firestone Art Collection (f 31)

Plate 33 *Shoreline, possibly Ellesmere Island*
5 x 8; likely July 31; private (njg 1694)

Plate 34 *Studies of Three Icebergs*
8 x 5; n.d.; private (njg 1366)

Plate 35 *Ellesmere Island, looking North from Craig Harbour*
circa 7 ¾ x 10 ⅞; August 2; Norman Mac-

kenzie Art Gallery, gift of the Artist; see plate 2, *A.Y.'s Canada* (njg 754)

Plate 36 *Glacier on Ellesmere, Rice Straits*
5 x 8, August; Winnipeg Art Gallery (njg 199)

Plate 37 *Ice Studies*
5 x 8; n.d.; private (njg 1365 verso)

Plate 38 *Sergeant White of the* RCMP, *and Across from Beechey*
8 x 5 and 5 x 8; August 5; private (f 1256)

Plate 39 *The Mary at Foot of Cliffs, Beechey Island*
7½ x 10⅞; August 6; Norman Mackenzie Art Gallery, gift of the Artist (njg 757)

Plate 40 *Beechey Island*
10⅞ x 7⅝; August 6; Norman Mackenzie Art Gallery, gift of A.Y. Jackson; compare Plate 11 of *The Far North* and Plate 6 and accompanying text of *A.Y.'s Canada* (njg 758)

Plate 41 *Beechey Island*
7½ x 10⅞; August 7; Firestone Art Collection (njg 38)

Plate 42 *Ice at Beechey Island*
5 x 8; August; Norman Mackenzie Art Gallery, gift of the Artist (njg 756)

Plate 43 *Inscription Carved into Stone at Port Leopold, Somerset Island*
circa 5 x 7⅝; August 8; private (njg 1257)

Plate 44 *Port Leopold, Somerset Island*
5½ x 9; August 9; private (njg 1674)

Plate 45 *Thule Eskimo Igloo Ruins, Port Leopold, Somerset Island*
7½ x 10½; August 9; Norman Mackenzie Art Gallery, gift of the Artist (njg 759)

Plate 46 *Admiralty Inlet*
7½ x 11; likely August 11; National Gallery of Canada, gift of A.Y. Jackson (NGC 17696/njg 194 verso)

Plate 47 *Admiralty Inlet*
7⅞ x 10⅞; August 11; later as 1930; private, Halifax (njg 193)

Plate 48 *Arctic Bay*
5 x 8; August; private (njg 195)

Plate 49 *Jumping the Ice Floes, Arctic Bay*
5 x 8; August; private; used as Plate 9a in *A.Y.'s Canada* with text from *The Far North* (njg 205)

Plate 50 *Arctic Bay: Eskimos Crossing the Ice Floes after Visiting the Beothic*
5 x 8; August; private; used as Plate 9b in

A.Y.'s Canada (njg 206 recto)

Plate 51 *Studies of Eskimos at Arctic Bay*
5 x 8; August; private (njg 206 verso)

Plate 52 *Baffin, North Shore near Navy Board*
7 ½ x 11; August; National Gallery of Canada, gift of A.Y. Jackson (NGC 17691/ njg 1277)

Plate 53 *Husky Dogs on Board the Beothic*
8 x 5; private; written on reverse side: 'I was getting pretty good at dogs. There were 50 on board the ship.' (njg 208)

Plate 54 *South Coast of Bylot Island*
7 ½ x 11; August 13; McMichael Canadian Collection; used for Plate 14 of *The Far North* (njg 191)

Plate 55 *Pond Inlet*
5 ½ x 9; August; private; oil sketch of same subject in Sarnia, acquired by Women's Art Conservation Association (njg 220)

Plate 56 *Pond Inlet, Baffin Island*
circa 7 ½ x 11; August 14; Norman Mackenzie Art Gallery, gift of the Artist (njg 760)

Plate 57 *Pond Inlet, Baffin Shore*
8 ⅜ x 10 ⅞; August; private, Halifax (njg 189 recto)

Plate 58 *Pond Inlet, Bylot Island in the Distance*
7 ⅝ x 11; August; Firestone Art Collection (f 39)

Plate 59 *Bylot from Pond Inlet*
7 ½ x 11; August; Firestone Art Collection; compare Plate 15 in *The Far North*, entitled 'Eclipse Sound at Pond Inlet' (f 29)

Plate 60 *Pond Inlet*
5 ½ x 9; August 16; private (njg 221)

Plate 61 *Mt. Morin, Pond's*
5 ½ x 9; August; private (njg 1675)

Plate 62 *Baffin South of Pond*
5 ½ x 9; n.d.; private (njg 1679)

Plate 63 *Large Berg*
7 ½ x 11; August 19; Alberta Art Foundation, Edmonton (njg 218 verso)

Plate 64 *North Shore, Cumberland Sound*
5 ½ x 9; August 21; private, (njg 219)

Plate 65 *Cumberland Sound*
7 ½ x 11; August; Alberta Art Foundation, Edmonton (njg 217 recto)

Plate 66 *Pangnirtung*
5 ½ x 9; August 22; private (njg 1667)

Plate 67   *Pangnirtung*
           5 ½ x 9; August 22; private (njg 1666)

Plate 68   *Pangnirtung*
           7 ⅜ x 11; August; private (njg 203)

Plate 69   *Hills of Pangnirtung*
           7 ½ x 11; n.d.; Norman Mackenzie Art Gallery, gift of the Artist (njg 762)

Plate 70   *Pyrola, Pangnirtung; Louse Wort and Heather, Lake Harbour*
           9 x 5 ½; August; private (njg 890)

Plate 71   *Studies of Eskimos in Kayaks, Godhavn and Pangnirtung*
           9 x 5 ½; n.d.; private (njg 1324)

Plate 72   *Inuit Figure Studies*
           8 x 5; August; private (njg 891)

Plate 73   *Pangnirtung*
           7 ½ x 11, with 1930 added later, incorrectly; Norman Mackenzie Art Gallery, gift of the Artist (njg 761)

Plate 74   *Entrance to Lake Harbour*
           5 x 8; August, with 1930 added later, incorrectly; private (njg 1507)

Plate 75   *Lake Harbour*
           5 ½ x 9; August; private (njg 1680)

Plate 76   *Port Burwell*
           7 ½ x 11; August; private, Sault Ste. Marie (Ontario) (njg 229)

Plate 77   *Moravian Mission at Port Burwell*
           9 x 7 ½; August; private (njg 1099)

Plate 78   *Two Sketches at Port Burwell*
           9 x 5 ½; August; private (njg 1689 recto)

Plate 79   *Captain Morin*
           9 x 5 ½; n.d.; private; this is a tracing of the original which Jackson gave to Captain Morin, the ice pilot (njg 1672)

Plate 80   *Portrait Studies on the Beothic, I*
           5 x 4 ⅝; n.d.; private (njg 1329)

Plate 81   *Portrait Studies on the Beothic, II*
           5 ½ x 9; August; private (njg 1328)

Plate 82   *On the Hatch of the Beothic*
           5 ½ x 9; Firestone Art Collection (f 40)

Plate 83   *Button Islands*
           5 ½ x 9; August 30/31; private (njg 1687)

Plate 84   *Cape Chidley*
           5 ½ x 9; August 31; private (njg 1681)

Plate 85   *Cape Chidley*

5 ½ x 9; August; private (njg 1683)

Plate 86 *Cape Chidley*
5 ½ x 9; August; private (njg 1684)

Plate 87 *Cape Chidley*
5 ½ x 9; August; private (njg 1685)

Plate 88 *Aurora Borealis over Labrador*
5 ½ x 9; September; private (njg 1688)

[introductory illustration]
Bylot Island
7 ³/₈ x 10 ¾; August 13; private collection, Ottawa (njg 190)

Date Due

APR. 16.1983			
DEC. 21.1993			
FEB 2 7 2001			

BRODART, INC. Cat. No. 23 233 Printed in U.S.A.